MARKET SYMPHONY

A Musician's Guide to Trading Stocks, ETFs, and Digital Assets

Market Symphony

Marcus G and Marcus Green

Published by The Triangle Royalty Group, 2026.

MARKET SYMPHONY

First edition. March 16, 2026.

ISBN: 979-8233695858

Written by Marcus G and Marcus Green.

Market Symphony

The Triangle Royalty Group LLC

Casa Grande, AZ

threepillars.tech

Disclaimer:

This book is designed to provide information and motivation to our readers. It is sold with the understanding that the publisher and author are not engaged to render any type of financial, legal, or professional advice. The content of this book is the sole expression and opinion of its author, and not necessarily that of the publisher. No warranties or guarantees are expressed or implied by the author's or publisher's choice to include any of the content in this volume. Neither the publisher nor the individual author shall be liable for any physical, psychological, emotional, financial, or commercial damages, including, but not limited to, special, incidental, consequential, or other damages.

Printed in the United States of America

First Edition: March 2026

Recording Vocals TRG Library Music @IDDC Studio Mix and Master Credits Fernando Bando

Dedication

This book is dedicated to the memory of my father, Johnathan Green.

Dad, I still remember watching the news with you as a child, mesmerized by those scrolling stock prices at the bottom of the screen. When I asked you what they were, you told me they were stock prices and asked if I had the money to buy some. At nine years old, with only three dollars in my pocket from doing chores, those numbers felt a world away—a mystery neither of us knew how to solve.

You taught me the value of a hard work ethic and the importance of climbing the economic ladder. Today, those scrolling numbers are no longer a mystery; they are the instruments in a symphony I have learned to conduct.

I also dedicate this to my wife, Michelle, for eighteen years of partnership, and to my seven children. You are the "why" behind every trade and the reason I strive to build a Sovereign Wealth Engine that will last for generations.

To the retail traders, the providers, and the dreamers: May this score help you find your own rhythm in the market.

A Letter to the Reader: Finding Your Rhythm

To the Provider, the Dreamer, and the Future Maestro:

Thank you for picking up this score. You are likely here because, like me, you've realized that the traditional "Wall Street" performance was never written with us in mind. For too long, the barrier to financial sovereignty was a high wall of complex jargon and "insider" gatekeeping.

When I started my career in 2007, I was an only child adopted by a hardworking family in Maryland. I didn't have a finance degree, but I had a work ethic and a lifelong love of music. I realized that the same discipline required to craft a drum pattern or compose a symphony is exactly what is needed to navigate the stock market.

I founded The Triangle Royalty Group (TRG) to be a "Sovereign Wealth Engine"—a way for retail traders to stop being passive listeners and start conducting their own financial destiny. This book is not a "get-rich-quick" scheme. It is a distillation of nearly 20 years of "rehearsals," including the painful "600 Dollar Lesson" that taught me the true meaning of risk management.

Whether you are a veteran, a parent, or someone simply looking for a "side-hustle" that can change your life, remember this: the market is a symphony of human emotion. If you can learn the notes, find the tempo, and stick to the plan, you can compose a legacy that lasts for generations.

Welcome to the orchestra. It's time to play.

Marcus Dewayne Green Sr. Founder, The Triangle Royalty Group LLC

Introduction

Thank you for taking the time to read this book. I greatly appreciate it. Countless hours have been dedicated to researching and compiling this information, driven by the hope of providing a valuable resource you can use throughout your life to generate income. Learning how to trade has been one of the most transformative skills I've acquired. It's been an ongoing journey, filled with challenges and rewards. This book is designed for traders at all levels, from complete novices to those seeking to refine existing strategies. It consolidates a wealth of information in one place, presented without bias and grounded in practical experience.

I will be selective in this book on my stock recommendations and my references to influencers and experts. This book merges insights from my personal experiences in the stock market with the collective wisdom of seasoned financial professionals. I've experienced financial setbacks—setbacks that were profoundly painful as a father of seven and the sole provider for my family. My hope is that by sharing my story, I can spare you from similar hardships.

We've all likely navigated periods of financial insecurity. The relentless struggle to get ahead can be incredibly daunting. The experience of losing a job despite unwavering dedication is deeply unsettling. Most of us could benefit from a little extra income. As a veteran of the United States Army, I firmly believe in the principle of KISS (Keep It Simple, Stupid) in all aspects of life. I will make every effort to adhere to this principle throughout this book.

While some financial concepts and terminology may initially seem intimidating, you will eventually discover a trading approach that aligns with your needs and propels you toward success.

While it is quite possible you can read this book in one sitting, I recommend using it as a reference guide throughout your investing career. This will help you retain the information better because you'll be using it in real-time. If you're new to trading, it may seem overwhelming to take in all this information. That's perfectly fine. Trading is not designed to be easy. If it were, there wouldn't be as much money to be made. Nothing worthwhile in life is easy. It becomes easier with practice and preparation.

Writing this book highlighted the general public's lack of trading knowledge. Unfortunately, this lack of knowledge is often exploited by seasoned traders. This book aims to level the playing field, empowering you with the knowledge and tools to navigate the markets confidently and achieve your financial goals.

Overture: Tuning the Instrument (Introduction)
- The Symphony of Income: Precision in Financial Markets
- The KISS Principle: Keeping the Composition Simple
- The Rehearsal: Using This Book as a Reference Guide

Part I: The Fundamentals of Composition (Chapters 1-2)

Chapter 1: The Score: Reading the Market's Intent (What You Will Gain From This Book)

- *Disclaimer: A Note of Caution*
- Beyond the Melody: Understanding Market Nuance
- The Conductor's Responsibility: Accessible Financial Literacy
- Crafting Your Unique Financial Tempo

Chapter 2: The Conductor's Journey: My Path to the Trading Pit (About Me – My Path to Trading)

- The Triangle Royalty Group: A Dedication to Financial Empowerment
- From Music to Markets: Discipline and the Long Game
- The Early Arrangements: My First Forays into Finance
- Finding the Right Rhythm: The Move to Swing Trading

Part II: Composing Your Financial Harmony (Chapters 3-4)

Chapter 3: Harmony: Composing the Financial Foundation (Foundations for Trading Success: Money, Discipline, and Self-Awareness)

- The Dual Nature of Money: Needs vs. Wants in the Financial Composition
- Prioritizing Needs: The Cornerstone of Financial Stability
- Introspection: The Conductor's Self-Awareness

Chapter 1: What You Will Gain From This Book

Disclaimer: *This information is for general knowledge and informational purposes only and does not constitute financial advice.*

My journey into the world of trading has been a deep dive, a constant quest for knowledge. I've devoured countless books and articles, listened to hours of interviews with market experts, and immersed myself in the vast ocean of financial information. My family might have thought I was a bit obsessed (and maybe they were right!), but I knew that if I wanted to truly succeed in trading, I had to dedicate myself fully to understanding it.

One of the recurring themes I encountered in my conversations about the stock market with people outside the world of finance was a focus on individual stock picks and the hope that their price would simply "go up." My response was always a gentle reminder: "That's a valid observation, but remember, prices can also go down." The stock market is far more nuanced than just identifying the next "hot stock." There's real potential for profit, but it requires a deep understanding of the underlying mechanics, the forces that drive market movements.

It quickly became apparent to me that much of this crucial information was simply not reaching a significant segment of the population. This wasn't a matter of race, gender, or any other arbitrary distinction. The dividing line was primarily economic. Working-class individuals with families, who struggle to accumulate the capital to even begin trading, and those in decent jobs who face the ever-present risk of corporate layoffs – both groups are often left vulnerable to financial instability. I thought about how this knowledge could empower my own family and friends, and the more I learned, the more I recognized the less-than-ethical tactics sometimes employed in the market. I felt a growing sense of responsibility to share this knowledge beyond my immediate circle. This information needs to be accessible to everyone.

This book is designed to provide you with the foundational principles of trading, a solid base upon which you can build your knowledge and refine your individual trading strategy. It consolidates essential information in a clear, unbiased, and authentic way. I won't be endorsing specific stocks or promoting particular investments. My focus is on empowering *you* to make informed decisions. I will, however, sparingly reference respected experts and influencers who have significantly contributed to the field of finance. This book blends essential market knowledge with insights gleaned from my own personal experiences in the trenches of the stock market. As a father of seven and the sole provider for my family, I've experienced the sting of financial losses – some of them deeply painful. My sincere hope is that by sharing these experiences, including the hard lessons learned, I can help you avoid similar financial hardships and navigate the market with greater resilience.

We've all likely faced periods of financial insecurity. The relentless struggle to get ahead can be incredibly disheartening. The experience of losing a job, despite hard work and dedication, can be devastating. The reality is that most of us could benefit from supplemental income, a way to build greater financial security and work towards our long-term goals. As a veteran of the United States Army, I firmly believe in the KISS principle – Keep It Simple, Stupid – and I've strived to adhere to this principle throughout this book. While some financial terms and concepts may initially seem intimidating, I'm confident that you'll eventually discover a trading system that aligns with your unique needs, risk tolerance, and aspirations for success.

My early forays into market research often led me down confusing and overwhelming rabbit holes of information. It was truly daunting. Despite my determination, I wasted valuable time and energy navigating these dead ends. I was diligently studying courses from prestigious institutions like Harvard and MIT (freely available on platforms like YouTube), while simultaneously encountering conflicting advice from individuals lacking real-world trading experience. I learned many lessons the hard way. This book will help you understand your own trading style, refine your trading skills, and connect you with exceptional mentors in the financial world who can guide you toward previously unimaginable success. Think of me not as a guru, but as a compass, pointing you in the right direction.

This book primarily focuses on trading stocks and ETFs. While some of the indicators and principles discussed can be applied to other markets, such as Forex and Cryptocurrency, the primary focus is on equities. It's also important to distinguish between trading (short-term strategies) and long-term investing (building a portfolio for the future). While there is some overlap, the approaches and mindsets are different.

Building a successful trading strategy is a highly personalized endeavor. There's no one-size-fits-all approach, and you'll find a wide array of tools and methods available to craft a strategy that perfectly aligns with your individual risk tolerance, financial goals, and available time commitment. This process of discovery and customization is crucial for long-term success.

One common misconception I've observed, particularly among those new to trading, is the desire for a "set it and forget it" system – a magic bullet that simply sends profitable trade alerts. The allure of passive income is understandable, but relying solely on alerts without understanding the underlying rationale is a recipe for potential disappointment. Blindly following trade recommendations without doing your own due diligence not only hinders your learning process but also puts your capital at significant risk. True passive income in trading isn't about passively receiving alerts; it's about developing a robust, well-researched strategy that you understand and can confidently execute. This involves understanding market dynamics, risk management, and the specific factors influencing your chosen assets.

It's paramount to understand that this book is for educational purposes only and does *not* constitute financial advice. I am not a financial advisor, and the information presented here should not be interpreted as specific stock recommendations or investment guidance. Building a sound financial plan requires the expertise of qualified professionals. I strongly encourage you to assemble a team of trusted advisors, including a financial advisor and a tax advisor. As your portfolio grows and your trading activities become more complex, the intricacies of tax planning, capital management, and estate planning demand professional attention. Trying to navigate these complexities alone can lead to costly mistakes.

This book aims to empower you with the knowledge and tools necessary to make informed trading decisions. It will guide you through the process of developing your own strategies, understanding risk, and navigating the complexities of the market. However, it's crucial to remember that this educational resource is not a substitute for personalized professional guidance. My goal is to help you develop the confidence and skills to achieve your financial objectives, but always within the framework of responsible financial planning and with the support of qualified advisors. Trading involves inherent risks, and it's essential to approach it with a clear understanding of those risks and a well-defined strategy.

Chapter 2: About Me – My Path to Trading

As the founder of The Triangle Royalty Group LLC, I'm driven by a passion to empower individual investors, helping them achieve their financial aspirations. This passion is deeply intertwined with my lifelong love of music. Just as music demands dedication, discipline, and an appreciation for the long game, so too does successful investing. Whether it's the intricate composition of a drum pattern or the strategic allocation of assets, I believe a deep understanding of fundamentals, combined with a patient and disciplined approach, is crucial for achieving lasting success. Like a musician meticulously crafting their sound, I advocate for a thoughtful and deliberate approach to investing, one that prioritizes building a strong foundation and cultivating long-term growth.

Through The Triangle Royalty Group LLC, I'm committed to providing valuable insights and resources to help fellow investors navigate the often-complex world of finance. My goal is to empower individuals to build that strong financial foundation and achieve their unique investment objectives, whether it's planning for a comfortable retirement, saving for a down payment on a dream home, or simply achieving greater financial freedom and peace of mind.

Continuous learning is a core value for me. I believe that the journey of investing is a lifelong pursuit, a continuous process of learning, adapting, and refining one's strategies. This is something you can pass down to your children. I'm dedicated to sharing my knowledge and experiences with others, fostering a community of informed and empowered investors who can support and learn from each other.

While I don't have a formal finance degree, I've always been drawn to the world of finance. About nine years ago, I briefly worked for a multi-level marketing (MLM) company focused on life insurance. This experience, though short-lived, ignited my interest in all things financial and provided me with a valuable introduction to the industry. During this time, I obtained my life insurance producers license, which further fueled my desire to learn more about financial products and strategies. This experience, though brief, helped me develop valuable skills in communication, problem-solving, and the ability to quickly grasp new concepts – skills that have proven invaluable in my trading career.

My personal investment journey began in 2007, when I was 27 years old and completely new to the world of finance. Growing up in Maryland, I, like many others, labored under the common misconception that investing was exclusively for the wealthy. This belief, while perhaps rooted in historical realities, began to shift with the rise of online trading platforms like E*TRADE in the early 1990s, which made investing more accessible to the average person.

I have a vivid childhood memory of watching the news with my dad, mesmerized by the scrolling numbers at the bottom of the screen while the news anchor talked about the stock market. I'd always ask my dad, "What are those numbers?" His standard reply was, "Those are stock prices, son. Why? Do you have money to buy some?" At the time, my financial resources consisted of maybe $3 from helping him with chores around the house. Looking at those stock prices, which seemed astronomically high to a child in the early 1990s, I felt a sense of disconnect. It seemed like investing was something completely out of reach. Adding to the mystery, neither I nor anyone in my family had any idea how to even buy a single share of stock.

This lack of financial education was a common experience for my generation. Despite the hard work ethic instilled in us, we received little to no formal instruction on investing or basic money management. The prevailing goal for most families was simply to buy a house – a decision that, in retrospect, could have significantly increased our long-term wealth.

Growing up, I witnessed many families striving to climb the economic ladder, moving from inner-city neighborhoods to the suburbs in search of better opportunities. This wasn't about race; it was about economic status. Financial resources dictated where you lived, with those who could afford it enjoying the relative comfort of the suburbs, while those with limited resources were often confined to inner-city housing projects or trailer parks. These early experiences instilled in me a deep understanding of the importance of financial literacy and the power of wealth building.

As an only child adopted by a hardworking family (a story for another time), I got an early taste of entrepreneurship. In elementary school, my friend Paul and I launched a small candy-selling business in 1988. We quickly learned the basics of supply and demand, and for two nine-year-olds, earning $10-$20 a day felt like a fortune. Our venture was short-lived, however, as the school swiftly shut down all candy-selling activities. This was my first encounter with business regulations – a valuable lesson in navigating constraints and adapting to changing circumstances.

Undeterred, we quickly pivoted, shifting our focus to supplying glue to a small group of students who actually ate the glue. While perhaps not the most ethical business model, it demonstrated our adaptability and willingness to explore alternative markets. These early entrepreneurial experiences, with their emphasis on identifying opportunities, navigating challenges, and adapting to setbacks, have profoundly influenced my approach to trading in the stock market.

Most of my adult life has been spent in project management, with a few years also working in the automotive industry as a General Manager. My wife and I have owned a Marketing and a Mobile Detailing business as well. Throughout these years, my investing was primarily focused on dividend stocks due to time constraints. I would diligently set aside a small portion of each paycheck or whatever I made that week and invest it in a diversified basket of dividend-paying stocks. I also dabbled in buying silver bullion as a hedge against inflation. While this approach provided a small, consistent return, I knew I wanted more from the markets. I watched the market daily. I recognized that billions of dollars flowed through the markets daily, and I was determined to participate more fully than just receiving a few dollars in dividends every quarter.

Driven by a desire to learn and grow, I explored various trading and investing styles. I tried them all, immersing myself in each one. In hindsight, I realize that if I had stuck with some of those styles a little longer, I likely could have achieved success. However, the style that resonated most deeply with me was swing trading. I felt that swing trading allowed me to leverage my skills in management, while also mitigating the emotional rollercoaster often associated with shorter-term trading strategies. I'd be remiss if I didn't acknowledge Gareth Soloway and his team at Verified Investing for laying a solid foundation for my current trading approach. Their guidance and insights were instrumental in shaping my understanding of the market.

MARKET SYMPHONY
A MUSICIAN'S GUIDE TO TRADING
STOCKS, ETFS, AND DIGITAL ASSETS

Chapter 3: Foundations for Trading Success: Money, Discipline, and Self-Awareness

Before diving into the exciting (and sometimes daunting) world of chart analysis and trading strategies, it's absolutely crucial to build a solid foundation of core principles. This chapter explores the essential and intertwined relationship between money management, unwavering discipline, and honest self-awareness – the bedrock upon which any successful trading journey is built. Without these foundational elements, even the most sophisticated technical analysis or trading system will likely fall short, leaving you vulnerable to the emotional and financial pitfalls that can derail even the most promising traders.

The Dual Nature of Money: Needs vs. Wants

Money, at its core, serves two fundamental purposes: meeting our basic needs and building wealth. Understanding this duality is paramount, especially for those venturing into the world of trading. The first purpose, acquiring essential goods and services – shelter, food, clothing, transportation – is self-evident. These are the non-negotiables, the foundation upon which we build our lives. However, the second purpose, building wealth, is where the potential of trading comes into play. Trading offers the opportunity to grow your capital beyond simply covering living expenses, enabling you to achieve long-term financial security, pursue your dreams, and ultimately attain financial freedom.

The challenge of building wealth and achieving financial independence is often less about the mechanics of investing and more about our complex, and often fraught, relationship with money. We live in a culture that bombards us with messages designed to stimulate our desire for immediate gratification. Advertising, social media, and even our social circles often reinforce the idea that happiness and success are tied to the acquisition of material possessions. This constant pressure to prioritize "wants" over "needs" creates a mindset that can be incredibly detrimental, especially when entering the world of trading.

The allure of quick profits and the potential for rapid wealth accumulation can be particularly seductive in this environment. However, trading requires discipline, patience, and a long-term perspective. Impulsive decisions driven by the desire for instant gratification, a trait often fueled by our consumerist culture, can quickly lead to substantial losses. The market doesn't reward emotional reactions; it rewards calculated risk assessment and strategic thinking. Someone constantly chasing the "next big thing" or trying to recoup losses quickly is far more likely to make poor decisions.

Here in the United States, the pervasive culture of instant gratification has significantly impacted how we manage our finances. Many households find themselves in a cycle of earning and spending, with little left over for saving or investing. This isn't necessarily a reflection of income level, but rather a consequence of prioritizing immediate gratification over long-term financial security. We see this manifested in a number of ways: from the constant upgrading of gadgets and the pursuit of fleeting trends, to the reliance on credit and the accumulation of debt. These patterns of behavior make it difficult to build the financial foundation necessary for successful trading. Before even considering the complexities of market analysis, individuals need to confront and address their own spending habits and cultivate a more disciplined approach to money management. This involves learning to differentiate between genuine needs and fleeting wants, developing a budget, and prioritizing saving and investing. Without this foundational work, even the most promising trading strategies are likely to be undermined by impulsive behavior and a lack of financial discipline.

Prioritizing Needs Over Wants: The Cornerstone of Financial Stability

Many of our everyday expenditures – the latest smartphone, entertainment subscriptions, frequent dining out, impulse purchases – often fall squarely into the category of *wants*, not *needs*. While these things can certainly enhance our lives and provide enjoyment, they're not essential for survival. It's easy to get caught up in the cycle of instant gratification, constantly seeking immediate pleasure through purchases. However, a critical step towards financial success, and particularly trading success, is developing the discipline to clearly distinguish between needs and wants.

Consider the stark reality faced by those living with limited resources. Their focus is, by necessity, on fulfilling basic needs. While this comparison might seem extreme, it serves as a powerful reminder of the importance of perspective and the need for mindful spending. Cultivating a sense of purpose and control over your finances is absolutely vital. This control empowers you to break free from the cycle of impulsive buying and allocate your resources strategically, including allocating a portion of your capital to the potentially rewarding, but also risky, endeavor of trading.

Humility and Self-Awareness: The Introspection Required for Trading Success

Effective trading demands a high degree of self-awareness. It's not enough to simply understand market trends or technical indicators; you must also understand *yourself*. Are you truly disciplined? Can you set realistic goals and consistently stick to them, even when faced with setbacks? Are you comfortable working independently, making critical decisions under pressure, and taking responsibility for the outcomes, both positive and negative? These are crucial questions to honestly ask yourself *before* embarking on a trading career.

If you struggle with discipline, goal setting, or independent work, trading might not be the right fit – at least not without significant personal development and a commitment to addressing these challenges. Trading requires consistency, a well-defined plan (your trading strategy), and the ability to execute that plan even when faced with losses, unexpected market fluctuations, or the temptation to deviate from your strategy based on emotions. It's akin to holding a demanding job where you must adhere to a strict schedule, complete tasks diligently, manage your time effectively, and be accountable for your performance. Without these qualities, your trading efforts are likely to be haphazard, inconsistent, and ultimately unsuccessful.

Mastering Money Management: The Bedrock of Trading Longevity

Strong money management is absolutely paramount for any trader, regardless of experience level. Losses are an inherent and unavoidable part of trading, especially for beginners. It's not a question of *if* you will experience losses, but *when* you will experience them and, more importantly, *how* you will manage them. Before risking even a small amount of capital in the market, ensure you have a substantial financial buffer in place to cover your essential needs (rent, food, utilities, etc.) for a reasonable period of time (ideally 3-6 months). This financial cushion provides a critical safety net, allowing you to weather market downturns and inevitable trading losses without jeopardizing your basic living expenses or adding undue stress to your life.

Financial stress is a major impediment to sound decision-making. If you're constantly worried about losing money that you need for rent or groceries, your judgment will be clouded by fear, and you'll be far more prone to emotional trading. Emotional trading, driven by fear or greed rather than logic and strategy, is a recipe for disaster. By establishing a solid foundation of financial stability, practicing responsible money management, and building a financial buffer, you create the mental and emotional space necessary to make rational, calculated trading decisions. This foundation is not just about protecting your capital; it's about protecting your ability to think clearly, manage risk effectively, and trade with discipline and confidence.

Chapter 4: Building Your Trading Foundation: From Financial Fitness to Mental Fortitude

My early experiences in the investment world drove home a crucial lesson: a well-defined strategy and a dedicated investment fund are absolutely essential. I learned the hard way that preserving capital is paramount. It's not about chasing the allure of quick wins or hitting the jackpot; it's about the steady, consistent process of building a sustainable portfolio that can weather market storms and deliver long-term growth. This requires careful planning, a clear understanding of your financial goals, and a healthy dose of realism.

Investing for Opportunities: Having the Resources to Act

A healthy financial reserve is absolutely crucial for seizing market opportunities when they arise. I've personally missed out on potentially profitable trades simply because I lacked the necessary funds at the right moment. It's a frustrating experience, like seeing a winning lottery ticket just out of reach. Resist the temptation to finance your trading activities with high-interest loans. The market demands respect, and that respect begins with responsible financial management. Cultivate the right mindset – one of patience, discipline, and long-term vision – *before* risking any significant capital.

Protecting Your Capital: The Personal Side of Investing (and Setting Boundaries)

The desire to share your investment journey with loved ones is understandable. You might be excited about your progress, eager to offer help, or simply want to discuss something you're passionate about. However, it's vital to recognize that sharing your investment plans can open a Pandora's Box of potential challenges:

- **Unsolicited Advice (and Pressure):** Even well-meaning family and friends might offer advice based on their own (often limited) understanding of investing. This advice, while given with good intentions, can be detrimental to your strategy. Furthermore, persistent unsolicited advice can create pressure to deviate from your plan, even if you know it's the wrong move.

- **Financial Requests and Obligations:** Sharing your investment successes (or even your plans) can lead to requests for loans, gifts, or financial assistance. While you may want to help your loved ones, mixing personal finances with family and friends can strain relationships and create awkward situations. Unexpected financial requests can also force you to liquidate investments prematurely, disrupting your strategy and potentially incurring losses.

- **Envy and Resentment:** Discussing your investment gains, especially if they're substantial, can sometimes trigger envy or resentment, even among those closest to you. This can create tension and damage relationships.

- **Misunderstandings and Misinterpretations:** Investing is complex, and it's easy for others to misinterpret your strategy or the risks involved. This can lead to unnecessary worry or even accusations of recklessness.

- **Loss of Control:** Once you've shared your plans, you've essentially invited others into your financial decision-making process. This can make it harder to stick to your strategy, especially when faced with external pressure or emotional appeals.

Setting Boundaries: A Crucial Skill

Protecting your capital and your peace of mind requires establishing clear boundaries. This doesn't mean being secretive or dishonest, but rather being selective about what you share and how you communicate about your investments:

- **Be Vague About Specifics:** Instead of detailing your portfolio holdings or specific trading strategies, talk about your overall financial goals and your long-term investment philosophy. For example, you could say, "I'm focusing on long-term growth through a diversified portfolio of stocks and bonds," rather than listing your individual stock picks.

- **Emphasize Risk Management:** Make it clear that investing involves risk and that losses are possible. This helps manage expectations and discourages others from viewing your investments as a guaranteed source of funds.

- **Politely Decline to Discuss Details:** If someone presses you for specifics, politely but firmly decline. You could say something like, "I appreciate your interest, but I'm not comfortable discussing the details of my investments. It's a personal matter, and I prefer to keep those details private."

- **Be Prepared to Say "No":** This is perhaps the most important boundary. Be prepared to say "no" to financial requests, even if it's uncomfortable. Explain that you have your own financial obligations and that you're committed to your long-term investment plan. You can offer alternative forms of support, such as helping them find a financial advisor or suggesting resources for financial education.

- **Lead by Example:** If you're genuinely interested in helping family and friends with their finances, focus on education rather than direct financial assistance. Share articles or resources on investing, budgeting, and financial planning. Encourage them to seek professional advice.

- **Focus on Your "Why":** Remind yourself why you're investing in the first place. Whether it's for retirement, your children's education, or financial independence, keeping your goals in mind can help you stay disciplined and resist external pressures.

One of the most challenging aspects of starting my trading journey was establishing clear financial boundaries, particularly within my family. It was difficult, initially, to say "no" to my wife when she had a request, even though she's never been one to desire extravagant possessions. I'm incredibly grateful for that. However, managing a household with seven children comes with significant daily expenses. Learning to distinguish between genuine needs and fleeting wants was a difficult but necessary lesson. Like many providers, I take pride in caring for my family, and saying "no" felt counterintuitive to that instinct.

I had to remind myself that my family is my ultimate "why," and that sometimes saying "no" in the short term is the best way to secure their long-term future. It wasn't about denying them necessities; it was about prioritizing our financial resources strategically. After completing my trading plan, my wife and I sat down and discussed it in detail. Open communication was essential. I wanted to clearly set expectations about my trading activities, the potential risks involved, and how it would fit into our overall financial picture. This transparency helped us both understand the bigger picture and work together toward our shared financial goals. It wasn't easy, but establishing these boundaries and having open conversations has been crucial for both our financial well-being and the success of my trading endeavors.

The Missed Opportunity Cost:

One of the biggest risks of not setting boundaries is the "missed opportunity cost." Imagine you've identified a promising trade, but you're forced to liquidate some of your holdings to cover an unexpected expense or fulfill a financial request. The missed gains from that trade can be substantial, and they represent a direct cost of not protecting your capital and setting boundaries.

Protecting your capital is not just about market analysis and risk management; it's also about managing the personal side of investing. Setting boundaries with family and friends is essential for maintaining control over your finances, avoiding unnecessary stress, and staying focused on your long-term goals. While sharing your investment journey can be tempting, remember that discretion is key. By being tactful but firm, you can protect your capital, preserve your relationships, and increase your chances of achieving your financial dreams.

Discipline is Key: The Unwavering Core of Trading Success

Trading is not a casual hobby; it's a demanding endeavor that requires unwavering discipline. Life will inevitably throw curveballs – unexpected expenses, family emergencies, personal challenges – but maintaining discipline in your trading approach is absolutely essential for long-term success. A lack of discipline can lead to impulsive decisions, emotional trading, and ultimately, significant financial losses, negating the very purpose of investing and jeopardizing your financial future.

Mastering Money Management: The Foundation of Financial Well-Being

Before you even consider buying your first stock or ETF, you *must* master the art of money management. This involves several key, interconnected steps:

1. Set Life Goals (with Specificity): Your Financial North Star

Generic financial advice rarely works. Your financial goals must be personalized, specific, and measurable. Consider both short-term goals (a down payment on a car, a dream vacation, paying off credit card debt) and long-term goals (retirement planning, homeownership, funding your children's education). Crucially, *quantify* these goals. Instead of simply saying "save for retirement," aim for something like "accumulate $1 million by age 65." This specificity provides a clear direction, strengthens your motivation, and allows you to track your progress effectively.

2. Create and Stick to a Budget: Your Financial Roadmap

Budgeting is the cornerstone of financial health. It's not about deprivation; it's about conscious spending and making your money work for you. A well-crafted budget allows you to track your income and expenses, identify areas where you can cut back on unnecessary spending, and stay on course toward your financial goals. The popular 50/30/20 rule can be a helpful starting point: 50% of your income is allocated to needs (rent, utilities, groceries), 30% to wants (entertainment, dining out, hobbies), and 20% to savings and debt repayment. Track *everything* – every expense, no matter how small. Use a spreadsheet, a budgeting app, or even a simple notebook. Regularly review your budget (monthly or quarterly) and make adjustments as needed. Your budget is not a static document; it's a dynamic tool that should evolve with your changing circumstances and priorities.

(Include a sample budget table here, similar to the one provided in the prompt, allowing space for users to fill in their own information.)

3. Pay Off All Debt: Freeing Yourself from Financial Shackles

Debt, especially high-interest debt (credit cards, payday loans, etc.), is a major obstacle to building wealth. It's like trying to run a race with weights tied to your ankles. Prioritize paying off debt aggressively. The example of a car loan with a 20% interest rate vividly illustrates the crippling effect of high-cost borrowing. Focus on *production* (investing, building assets), not just *consumption*. Prioritizing debt repayment frees up income that can then be channeled towards more productive purposes, such as investing and growing your wealth. Consider different debt repayment strategies, such as the "snowball method" (paying off the smallest debt first for motivation) or the "debt avalanche method" (paying off the debt with the highest interest rate first to minimize overall interest costs).

4. Living Below Your Means: The Path to Financial Freedom and Flexibility

Living below your means is a fundamental principle of long-term financial success. It simply means spending less money than you earn, consistently. This practice allows you to save more, avoid accumulating unnecessary debt, and ultimately achieve financial stability and freedom. It's not about sacrificing all enjoyment in life; it's about conscious spending, making informed choices, and aligning your expenses with your income and your financial goals. Start small, involve your family in the process (making it a team effort), and utilize technology (budgeting apps, meal planning tools) to your advantage. Find a healthy balance between frugality and enjoying the things that truly matter to you.

5. Building an Emergency Fund: Your Financial Safety Net

Once you've established a solid habit of living below your means, the next crucial step is building an emergency fund. This fund should ideally cover 3-6 months of essential living expenses (rent/mortgage, utilities, food, transportation, etc.) and provide a financial cushion against unexpected events – job loss, medical emergencies, car repairs, or any other unforeseen circumstances that could disrupt your financial stability. Having an emergency fund not only protects you financially but also provides peace of mind, allowing you to trade and invest with less stress and emotional pressure.

The Importance of Physical and Mental Well-Being: The Trader's Edge

Finally, it's essential to recognize the powerful connection between your physical and mental health and your success as a trader. Physical health directly impacts your focus, concentration, energy levels, and discipline – all vital qualities for effective trading. Mental health plays an even more significant role, influencing your emotional regulation (managing fear and greed), your risk management (making rational decisions), your resilience (bouncing back from losses), and your overall confidence in your trading abilities. Prioritize self-care: make time for regular physical activity, practice mindfulness or meditation to manage stress, cultivate positive and supportive relationships, and don't hesitate to seek professional help from a therapist or counselor if you're struggling with mental health challenges.Investing in your physical and mental well-being is not a luxury; it's an investment in your overall success, both in trading and in life. A healthy body and a clear, focused mind are essential tools for navigating the complexities of the market and achieving your financial goals

Trading is a demanding endeavor, requiring intense focus, quick decision-making under pressure, and the ability to manage significant emotional swings. Both physical and mental health play critical roles in supporting these demands:

- **Physical Health: Fueling Peak Performance:**
  - **Focus and Concentration:** Poor physical health can lead to fatigue, brain fog, and difficulty concentrating, making it hard to analyze charts, identify opportunities, and execute trades effectively.
  - **Energy Levels:** Trading can be mentally draining. Maintaining good physical health through proper diet, exercise, and sleep ensures you have the energy to stay alert and focused throughout the trading day.
  - **Discipline and Stamina:** Physical activity promotes discipline and resilience, qualities that are essential for sticking to your trading plan and managing losses.
  - **Stress Management:** Regular exercise is a powerful stress reliever, helping you manage the anxiety and pressure that come with trading.
- **Mental Health: The Inner Game of Trading:**
  - **Emotional Regulation:** Trading involves dealing with both wins and losses. Strong mental health allows you to manage fear and greed, preventing impulsive decisions driven by emotions.
  - **Risk Management:** Rational decision-making is crucial for effective risk management. Mental clarity and emotional stability enable you to assess risks objectively and avoid reckless trades.
  - **Resilience:** Losses are inevitable in trading. Mental resilience helps you bounce back from setbacks, learn from your mistakes, and avoid letting losses derail your overall strategy.
  - **Confidence:** A healthy mindset fosters confidence in your trading abilities, allowing you to execute your plan with conviction and avoid second-guessing yourself.

○ **Stress Management:** Trading can be highly stressful. Mental health practices like mindfulness, meditation, and therapy can equip you with tools to manage stress effectively.

Prioritizing Self-Care: Investing in Your Trading Edge:

Taking care of your physical and mental well-being is not a luxury; it's an investment in your trading success. Here are some practical steps you can take:

- **Regular Physical Activity:** Aim for at least 30 minutes of moderate-intensity exercise most days of the week. Find activities you enjoy, whether it's running, swimming, yoga, or weightlifting.

- **Balanced Diet:** Fuel your body with nutritious foods, including plenty of fruits, vegetables, whole grains, and lean protein. Avoid processed foods, sugary drinks, and excessive caffeine.

- **Adequate Sleep:** Prioritize getting 7-9 hours of quality sleep each night. Sleep deprivation can impair cognitive function and increase stress levels.

- **Mindfulness and Meditation:** Practicing mindfulness or meditation can help you manage stress, improve focus, and cultivate emotional awareness. Even a few minutes a day can make a difference.

- **Stress Management Techniques:** Explore various stress management techniques, such as deep breathing exercises, progressive muscle relaxation, or spending time in nature.

- **Cultivate Supportive Relationships:** Surround yourself with positive and supportive people who understand the challenges of trading.

- **Seek Professional Help:** Don't hesitate to seek professional help from a therapist or counselor if you're struggling with mental health challenges. There's no shame in asking for help, and it can be a sign of strength.

The Trader's Edge: A Holistic Approach:

True trading success comes from a holistic approach that integrates sound trading strategies with peak physical and mental well-being. When you're physically and mentally healthy, you're better equipped to:

- **Make rational decisions:** You're less likely to be swayed by emotions like fear or greed.

- **Stick to your trading plan:** You have the discipline and focus to execute your strategy consistently.

- **Manage risk effectively:** You can assess risks objectively and avoid impulsive trades.

- **Learn from your mistakes:** You have the mental clarity to analyze your trades and identify areas for improvement.

- **Handle stress and pressure:** You're more resilient in the face of market volatility and setbacks.

Investing in your physical and mental well-being is not just a good idea; it's an *essential* part of becoming a successful trader. By prioritizing self-care, you're not only improving your overall quality of life but also giving yourself a significant edge in the market. A healthy body and a clear, focused mind are invaluable assets in the world of trading, enabling you to navigate its complexities with greater confidence, resilience, and ultimately, success.

I was unable to "enhance a photo" because the selected item is a table placeholder in your document, not an image.

Category	Recommended % of Income (50/30/20 Rule)	Your Monthly Budget	Your Actual Spending	Difference
Needs (50%)				
Housing (Rent/Mortgage)				
Utilities				
Groceries				
Transportation/Car Payment				
Insurance				
Wants (30%)				
Entertainment				
Dining Out				
Hobbies/Shopping				
Vacation Fund				
Savings & Debt Repayment (20%)				
Emergency Fund				
Investments/Trading Capital				

High-Interest Debt Repayment	
Total	**100%**

Chapter 5: The Origin and Nature of Currency: A Foundation for Investors

You have picked this book up because you want to make more money. But what is money?

In the United States, the Federal Reserve (often called "the Fed") plays a crucial role in managing the nation's monetary system. It's a complex institution, and a basic understanding of its function is vital for any serious investor. I encourage you to explore the Fed's role further through reputable sources (many excellent books and articles are available), but I'll provide a brief overview based on publicly available information.

The Federal Reserve was established in 1913 as a response to a series of financial panics, most notably the Panic of 1907. These crises demonstrated the need for a central authority to manage the money supply, regulate banks, and prevent future financial collapses. The Federal Reserve Act, signed into law by President Woodrow Wilson, created this institution.

The Fed's primary goals are to stabilize the American banking system, mitigate financial crises, promote maximum employment, and maintain stable prices (controlling inflation). Its structure consists of the Board of Governors (an independent government agency in Washington, D.C.) and 12 regional Federal Reserve Banks. The Fed's responsibilities are broad, including setting monetary policy (influencing interest rates and the money supply), regulating banking institutions, maintaining financial system stability, and providing financial services to banks and the government.

Currency: The Lifeblood of the Economy (and Your Trading)

Understanding the origin of currency is important, but even more crucial is grasping its dynamic nature. I prefer the term "currency" because it emphasizes the constant flow and exchange of money within the economy. Think about the sheer volume of transactions happening every second of every day, from your morning coffee purchase to multi-million dollar trades involving publicly traded companies – the very companies you might be investing in.

As an investor and trader, you're not just looking at numbers on a screen; you're trying to decipher the flow of currency. Where is it going? Where is it coming from? This knowledge is invaluable. It provides critical insights into economic trends, information that major corporations invest vast resources to uncover. You can find all of this information in stock or ETFs charts with basic indicators. By understanding the forces that drive the flow of currency, you can gain a significant edge in the market.

The Flow of Currency and Its Impact on the Stock Market

The stock market isn't an isolated entity; it's intricately connected to the broader economy and the flow of currency. Here are some key ways this flow directly impacts your trading:

- Interest Rates: The Fed's decisions regarding interest rates have a profound and immediate impact on the stock market. Lower interest rates generally make borrowing cheaper, encouraging businesses to expand and consumers to spend, which can boost stock prices. Conversely, higher interest rates can have the opposite effect, making borrowing more expensive and potentially slowing economic growth.

- Inflation: Inflation, the rate at which prices rise over time, can erode the value of money. High inflation can make investors nervous, leading them to sell stocks and seek safer havens, potentially triggering market downturns. The Fed's efforts to control inflation are therefore closely watched by investors and traders.

- Economic Growth: A healthy and growing economy generally leads to increased corporate profits, which in turn drives stock prices higher. The flow of currency is a key driver of economic growth, influencing investment, production, and consumer spending.

- Investor Sentiment: The flow of currency can also significantly impact investor sentiment. For example, a sudden influx of foreign capital into the U.S. stock market might signal confidence in the U.S. economy, encouraging further investment and driving up stock prices. Conversely, a sudden outflow of capital can create fear and uncertainty, potentially triggering a sell-off.

- Currency Exchange Rates: For companies that do business internationally, currency exchange rates can have a significant impact on their profitability and therefore their stock prices. Fluctuations in exchange rates can also create trading opportunities in the currency market itself.

Connecting the Dots: From Currency Flow to Your Trading Decisions

Understanding the flow of currency isn't just an abstract economic concept; it has very practical implications for your trading decisions. By paying close attention to economic indicators (GDP growth, unemployment rates, inflation data), Fed announcements, and other factors that influence the flow of currency, you can gain a deeper understanding of market trends and make more informed trading choices. Each one of the reports has some sort of relationship to the stock market.

For example, if you see signs that the economy is slowing down and the Fed is likely to lower interest rates, you might consider investing in sectors that are more sensitive to interest rates, such as real estate, technology, or consumer discretionary stocks. Conversely, if you anticipate rising inflation, you might look for investments that can provide a hedge against inflation, such as commodities, precious metals, or real estate.

In short, understanding the flow of currency is essential for navigating the complexities of the stock market. It's not just about picking the right stocks; it's about understanding the broader economic context in which those stocks operate. By developing a keen awareness of the forces that drive the flow of currency, you can significantly improve your chances of trading success. This knowledge allows you to anticipate market movements, identify potential risks and opportunities, and make more informed decisions about when to enter and exit trades.

Chapter 6: Navigating the Markets: Understanding Investing, Trading, and Your Role as a Retail Trader

This chapter provides a comprehensive overview of investing, differentiates it from trading, explores the various ways people invest, and specifically defines what it means to be a retail trader navigating today's dynamic financial markets.

What is Investing? The Long Game

Investing, at its core, is about strategically allocating resources – whether financial capital, time, or effort – with the expectation of generating future benefits. In the financial realm, investing typically involves deploying capital into assets like stocks, bonds, real estate, or other investment vehicles with the primary goal of generating returns over the *long term*. It's a process of planting seeds today and patiently nurturing their growth, understanding that the real rewards, like a mature tree bearing fruit, may take considerable time to fully materialize. This long-term perspective is a crucial distinction between investing and trading.

Think of the process like cultivating a thriving orchard. You begin with carefully selected seeds (your initial investments), nurture their growth with consistent care – watering (regular contributions), fertilizing (rebalancing your portfolio), and protecting them from harm (managing risk). While the initial investment may seem small, with time, patience, and consistent effort, the orchard matures, providing shade, shelter, and a bountiful harvest. Similarly, the power of compound interest, where your earnings generate further earnings, allows financial investments to grow exponentially over time. However, this growth requires sustained discipline, a long-term perspective, and the ability to resist the temptation to harvest prematurely.

Investing is typically driven by a combination of motivations:

- Growth: The potential for capital appreciation, where your initial investment increases in value over time. This could be through rising stock prices, increasing property values, or the growth of a business.

- Income: Generating a regular stream of income through dividends (from stocks), interest payments (from bonds), rental income (from real estate), or other income-generating assets.

- Beating Inflation: Preserving and increasing your purchasing power by ensuring your investments outpace the rate of inflation, which erodes the value of money over time.

- Financial Security: Building a financial safety net and accumulating wealth for long-term goals like retirement, funding education, purchasing a home, or achieving financial independence.

How People Invest: A Diverse Range of Options

The world of investing offers a diverse range of options, each with its own risk and reward profile. Understanding these different asset classes is crucial for building a well-diversified portfolio:

- Stocks (Equities): Represent ownership in a publicly traded company. Stocks offer the highest potential returns but also carry the highest risk. Stock prices can fluctuate significantly based on company performance, economic conditions, and investor sentiment.

- Bonds (Fixed Income): Represent a loan to a company or government. Bonds generally offer lower returns than stocks but are considered less risky. Bond prices are less volatile than stock prices and are often influenced by interest rate changes.

- Real Estate: Investing in physical property, such as residential or commercial buildings, for rental income or potential appreciation in value. Real estate can be a good long-term investment but is less liquid than stocks or bonds.

- Mutual Funds: Pools of money from multiple investors, managed by professional fund managers and invested in a diversified portfolio of assets (stocks, bonds, or a combination). Mutual funds offer instant diversification and professional management but come with management fees.

- Exchange-Traded Funds (ETFs): Similar to mutual funds in that they hold a basket of assets, but ETFs are traded on stock exchanges like individual stocks, offering greater flexibility and lower fees than many mutual funds.

- Alternative Investments: This category includes a wide range of assets, such as hedge funds, private equity, commodities (gold, oil, etc.), and cryptocurrencies. These investments can offer diversification and potentially high returns but often come with higher risk and less liquidity.

- Tax-Advantaged Accounts: Retirement accounts like 401(k)s and IRAs, offering tax benefits to encourage saving and investing for retirement. These accounts can hold a variety of investments, such as stocks, bonds, and mutual funds.

What is Trading? Capitalizing on Short-Term Market Movements

Trading, in contrast to investing, focuses on capitalizing on *short-term* price fluctuations in financial markets. Traders actively buy and sell securities – stocks, options, futures, currencies, etc. – within a much shorter timeframe, ranging from days or weeks to even minutes or seconds (in the case of day trading and high-frequency trading). The goal is to profit from these short-term price swings, rather than holding assets for the long term. While trading can potentially generate quicker profits than long-term investing, it also involves significantly higher risk and requires a different skill set. Trading, unlike its long-term counterpart investing, is similar to surfing. Imagine a surfer, not patiently waiting for the perfect, massive wave to ride for miles, but instead, skillfully navigating the smaller, more frequent swells closer to shore. These smaller waves, while not as grand, offer constant opportunities for movement, for action, for potential reward. That's the essence of trading – capitalizing on the short-term fluctuations in the financial markets, riding the waves of price movement rather than waiting for the tide to turn in your favor over years.

Traders are active participants in the market, constantly engaged in buying and selling securities – stocks, options, futures, currencies, commodities, and a myriad of other financial instruments. Their time frame is significantly shorter than that of an investor. While an investor might hold a stock for years, a trader might hold the same stock for days, weeks, hours, or even minutes. Day traders, the most active of the bunch, might open and close multiple positions *within the same trading day*, never holding anything overnight. High-frequency traders, using sophisticated algorithms and lightning-fast computers, operate on time frames measured in milliseconds, exploiting tiny price discrepancies that vanish in the blink of an eye.

The enticement of trading lies in the potential for quicker profits. Imagine catching a series of these smaller waves, each ride bringing you closer to your destination faster than waiting for one giant wave. This potential for rapid returns is what draws many to the world of trading. However, this potential reward comes with a significant caveat: *risk*.

Think of our surfer again. Riding those smaller, more frequent waves is inherently more precarious than waiting for the big one. The smaller waves are choppier, less predictable, and can easily wipe you out if you're not skilled and attentive. Similarly, trading involves significantly higher risk than long-term investing. Market conditions can change rapidly, news events can trigger sudden price swings, and a trader must be prepared to react quickly and decisively.

The Trader's Mindset: Skill, Discipline, and Adaptability

Trading requires a unique skillset, quite different from that of an investor. It's not about picking a company you believe in and holding it for the long haul. It's about understanding market dynamics, analyzing price charts, recognizing patterns, and making calculated decisions based on probabilities, not hopes. It's about being able to detach emotionally from the market, to avoid letting fear or greed cloud your judgment.

A trader must have the discipline to stick to their trading plan, to cut losses quickly when a trade goes wrong, and to resist the temptation to chase profits. Adaptability is also essential. The market is constantly evolving, and traders must be able to adapt their strategies to changing conditions.

A Story from the Trading Floor:

Picture a bustling trading floor, the air thick with tension and excitement. Traders are glued to their screens, monitoring price movements, analyzing charts, and executing trades with rapid-fire precision. A young trader named Jacob, fresh out of college, has just placed a trade on a promising tech stock. The stock price surges, and he feels a rush of adrenaline. He's tempted to hold on, hoping for even bigger gains. But then, he remembers his training. His mentor had drilled into him the importance of discipline and risk management. Jacob had set a target profit and a stop-loss level for the trade. He takes a deep breath, resists the urge to gamble, and closes the position, locking in his profit.

Later that day, the same stock price plummets on news of a product recall. The young trader is grateful for his discipline. If he had let greed cloud his judgment and hadn't set a stop-loss, he would have suffered a significant loss. He learned a valuable lesson that day: in the world of trading, discipline and risk management are just as important as identifying profitable opportunities.

Trading is a dynamic and demanding activity that focuses on capitalizing on short-term market movements. It offers the potential for quicker profits but involves significantly higher risk and requires a different skillset than long-term investing. Successful traders possess a combination of analytical skills, discipline, adaptability, and emotional control. They understand the importance of risk management and are prepared to react quickly and decisively to changing market conditions. It's a high-stakes game, but for those with the right mindset and skillset, it can be a rewarding pursuit.

What is a Retail Trader? You Are Now an Active Participant

A retail trader is an individual who trades financial instruments for their own personal account, using their own capital, rather than on behalf of a financial institution. You, as an individual investor making your own trading decisions, are a retail trader. We, collectively, *are* the market. Our combined buy and sell orders, our collective sentiment, and our reactions to market news and events influence price movements and shape the overall market landscape.

The accessibility of retail trading is incredibly empowering. Anyone with a relatively small amount of capital and an internet connection can now participate in the financial markets. This democratization of finance has opened up opportunities for individuals to take control of their financial future. However, it's crucial to recognize that the playing field is not entirely level. Large institutional investors, like hedge funds and investment banks, have access to vast resources, sophisticated trading platforms, advanced analytical tools, and often possess information that is not readily available to the average retail trader. This information asymmetry can be a significant disadvantage and is the reason for this book.

Retail traders have to follow certain rules. The Securities and Exchange Commission (SEC) has rules in place to regulate day trading activities, primarily focusing on investor protection and market integrity. Here's a breakdown of the key SEC rules for day traders:

1. Pattern Day Trader Rule:

- **Definition:** The Financial Industry Regulatory Authority (FINRA), under SEC oversight, defines a "pattern day trader" as any customer who executes four or more day trades within five business days, provided that these day trades represent more than 6% of the customer's total trading activity in their margin account during that same period.

- **Margin Requirements:** Pattern day traders are subject to specific margin requirements:

  - **Minimum Equity:** They must maintain a minimum equity of $25,000 in their margin account on any day they day trade. This amount must be in the account before any day trading activities and must be maintained at all times.

  - **Day Trading Buying Power:** Pattern day traders can trade up to four times their maintenance margin excess as of the close of the previous business day.

  - **Margin Calls:** If a pattern day trader exceeds their day trading buying power limitation, their broker-dealer will issue a day trading margin call. The trader then has five business days to meet this call.

  - **Restrictions:** Failure to meet a margin call can lead to further restrictions on the account, including being limited to cash transactions for 90 days.

2. General Margin Rules:

- Day trading typically involves margin accounts, which allow traders to borrow money from their broker to trade.

- The SEC's Regulation T governs the initial margin requirements for securities transactions, setting the minimum percentage of the purchase price that must be paid in cash.

3. Anti-Manipulation Rules:

- The SEC has strict rules against market manipulation, including practices like "pump and dump" schemes, where traders artificially inflate the price of a security to profit from its subsequent decline.

- Day traders must be aware of these rules and avoid any activities that could be construed as manipulative.

4. Insider Trading:

- Insider trading, the buying or selling of securities based on non-public information, is illegal.

- Day traders must ensure they are not trading on inside information.

5. Record Keeping:

- Broker-dealers are required to keep detailed records of customer transactions, including day trades.

- Day traders should also maintain their own records of their trading activities.

Important Considerations for Day Traders:

- **Risk:** Day trading is inherently risky and can lead to significant financial losses. The SEC emphasizes that day trading is generally not appropriate for individuals with limited resources, limited investment or trading experience, and low-risk tolerance.

- **Education:** Day traders should have a thorough understanding of the markets, trading strategies, and risk management techniques.

- **Broker-Dealer Rules:** Broker-dealers may have their own specific rules and requirements for day traders, which may be stricter than the SEC's regulations.

Leveraging Your Unique Perspective: The "Boots on the Ground" Advantage

However, as a retail trader, you also have certain unique advantages. Being outside the "Wall Street bubble" gives you direct access to real-world consumer trends and behaviors. You see firsthand what products are gaining popularity, what services are in demand, and what truly matters to consumers in their daily lives. This "boots on the ground" perspective can be invaluable, providing insights that Wall Street analysts, often focused on macroeconomic data, might miss. They also spend millions on researching these trends. Even seemingly mundane activities, like a trip to the grocery store, can become a valuable research opportunity. Pay attention to brands, examine product labels, and then research the companies behind those products.

The Importance of Research, Discipline, and a Well-Defined Strategy

"Research" is a broad term, encompassing a multitude of activities. There's no single "right" way to conduct research; the key is to develop a process that works for you. This book will provide you with a solid foundation of knowledge, but it's essential to continuously learn and adapt as the markets evolve. Don't feel overwhelmed by the sheer volume of information available. It's tempting to try to absorb everything at once, but that's a recipe for information overload and analysis paralysis.

One of the most common pitfalls for new traders is a lack of focus and discipline. It's easy to get caught up in the excitement of potential profits and jump from one trading strategy to another, chasing the latest "hot tip" or indicator. This "shiny object syndrome" can be detrimental to your trading success. My early trading experiences were marked by this lack of focus. I'd flit from one strategy to another, never giving any single approach enough time to prove itself. This is a classic mistake.

The key is to develop a well-defined trading strategy, based on thorough research and analysis, and then *stick to it*. Discipline is absolutely paramount. Even the most successful traders will experience losing streaks. That's the inherent nature of probability and risk. Every trade carries the potential for loss. Thorough research is crucial to identify favorable entry points and set realistic price targets (your profit targets and stop-loss levels). And if a trade doesn't go as planned, don't hesitate to exit the position. Resist the urge to "force" a trade based on emotions, hope, or a "gut feeling." Successful trading requires a combination of knowledge, discipline, patience, a well-defined strategy, and a realistic understanding of risk. It's a skill that takes time and effort to develop, but the rewards can be significant for those who are willing to put in the work.

Chapter 7: Decoding the Language of Trading: A Glossary of Essential Terms

Navigating the world of trading is like learning a new language. It has its own vocabulary, its own set of rules, and its own unique way of communicating. This chapter serves as your essential guide to the key terms and definitions used in the trading world. Understanding these concepts is absolutely crucial for comprehending market dynamics, making informed trading decisions, and effectively communicating with other traders and financial professionals. This glossary will be a valuable reference throughout your trading journey, empowering you to confidently navigate the complexities of the financial markets.

A

• **Alpha:** A measure of an investment's performance relative to a benchmark index. A positive alpha indicates that the investment has outperformed the benchmark, while a negative alpha suggests underperformance. *Example:* If a stock has an alpha of 2, it means it has outperformed its benchmark by 2%.

• **Asset Allocation:** The process of dividing your investment funds among different asset classes (stocks, bonds, real estate, commodities, etc.) to optimize risk and return. A well-diversified asset allocation strategy is crucial for managing risk and achieving your long-term financial goals. *Example:* A common asset allocation might be 60% stocks and 40% bonds.

• **Accrued Interest:** Interest that has accumulated on a bond or other debt instrument but has not yet been paid out. This is important to understand when buying or selling bonds between interest payment dates.

B

• **Beta:** A measure of a stock's volatility relative to the overall market. A beta of 1 indicates that the stock's price tends to move in line with the market. A beta greater than 1 suggests higher volatility (the stock's price will fluctuate more than the market), while a beta less than 1 indicates lower volatility. *Example:* A stock with a beta of 1.2 is considered more volatile than the market.

• **Bear Market:** A market condition characterized by falling prices (typically a decline of 20% or more from a recent peak) and pessimistic investor sentiment.

• **Blue-Chip Stock:** A stock of a large, well-established, and financially sound company with a long history of consistent dividend payments and stable earnings. Blue-chip stocks are generally considered less risky than smaller, less established companies. *Example:* Companies like Coca-Cola, Microsoft, and Johnson & Johnson are often considered blue-chip stocks.

• **Bond:** A debt security issued by a corporation or government entity to raise capital. Bondholders are essentially lending money to the issuer and receive regular interest payments (coupon payments) in return, along with the return of their principal at maturity.

• **Bond Yield:** The annual return on a bond, expressed as a percentage. The yield takes into account the bond's current market price, its coupon rate, and its time to maturity.

• **Bull Market:** A market condition characterized by rising prices (typically a gain of 20% or more from a recent trough) and optimistic investor sentiment.

• **Bull Trap:** A false upward movement in a downtrend, often leading to losses for traders who enter long positions (betting that the price will rise).

C

• **Capital Gains:** The profit realized from the sale of an asset, such as a stock or property, when the selling price is higher than the purchase price.

• **Compounding:** The process of earning interest on both the principal amount and the accumulated interest from previous periods. Compounding is a powerful force for wealth creation over the long term. *Example:* Investing $1,000 at a 7% annual return will earn you $70 in interest the first year. The second year, you'll earn 7% on $1,070 ($1,000 principal + $70 interest), and so on.

• **Commodities:** Tangible assets such as gold, oil, natural gas, and agricultural products (corn, wheat, soybeans). Commodities are often traded on futures exchanges.

• **Credit Rating:** An assessment of the creditworthiness of a borrower (individual, company, or government), typically expressed as a letter grade (e.g., AAA, AA, A, BBB, etc.). Higher credit ratings indicate lower risk of default.

• **Currency:** The unit of money used in a particular country or economic region. *Example:* The U.S. dollar, the Euro, the Japanese yen.

• **Currency Exchange Rate:** The price of one currency expressed in terms of another currency. Exchange rates fluctuate constantly based on supply and demand, economic conditions, and geopolitical events.

D

• **Deflation:** A general decline in prices for goods and services within an economy. Deflation can lead to economic stagnation as consumers postpone purchases in anticipation of further price declines.

• **Derivative:** A financial instrument whose value is *derived* from an underlying asset, such as a stock, bond, commodity, or currency. Options and futures contracts are examples of derivatives.

• **Discount Rate:** The interest rate at which commercial banks can borrow money directly from the Federal Reserve. The discount rate influences other interest rates throughout the economy.

• **Diversification:** Spreading investments across different asset classes, sectors, and geographic regions to reduce overall portfolio risk. Diversification helps to protect your portfolio from the negative impact of any single investment performing poorly.

• **Dividend:** A portion of a company's profits that is distributed to its shareholders. Dividends are typically paid out quarterly.

• **Dividend Yield:** The annual dividend per share divided by the stock price. The dividend yield represents the return on investment from dividends alone.

• **Dow Jones Industrial Average (DJIA):** A price-weighted index of 30 large, publicly owned companies listed on U.S. stock exchanges. The DJIA is often used as a benchmark to measure the overall performance of the U.S. stock market.

E

• **Earnings Per Share (EPS):** A company's net income divided by the number of outstanding shares. EPS is a key metric used to evaluate a company's profitability.

- **Emerging Markets:** Countries with developing economies that are experiencing rapid growth. Emerging markets offer high growth potential but also carry higher risk due to political instability, currency fluctuations, and less developed financial systems.

- **Equities:** Another term for stocks or shares of ownership in a company.

- **Exchange-Traded Fund (ETF):** A basket of securities (stocks, bonds, commodities) that trades on a stock exchange like a single stock. ETFs offer diversification, low costs, and liquidity.

F

- **Federal Deposit Insurance Corporation (FDIC):** A U.S. government corporation that insures deposits in banks up to a certain amount, protecting depositors from losses in the event of bank failure.

- **Federal Reserve (The Fed):** The central banking system of the United States, responsible for monetary policy (controlling the money supply and interest rates).

- **Financial Planning:** The process of creating a comprehensive plan for managing your finances, including budgeting, saving, investing, retirement planning, and estate planning.

- **Foreign Exchange (Forex):** The global market for the trading of currencies. Forex trading is the largest and most liquid financial market in the world.

- **Futures Contract:** An agreement to buy or sell an asset (commodity, currency, or financial instrument) at a specified price on a future date. Futures contracts are traded on futures exchanges.

G

- **Growth Stock:** A stock of a company that is expected to experience rapid earnings growth. Growth stocks often have high P/E ratios and may not pay dividends.

H

- **Hedge Fund:** A privately managed investment fund that uses a variety of strategies, often employing leverage and complex investment techniques, to generate returns for its investors. Hedge funds typically cater to high-net-worth individuals and institutional investors.

I

- **Inflation:** The rate at which the general level of prices for goods and services is rising, eroding the purchasing power of money.

- **Initial Public Offering (IPO):** The first sale of stock by a private company to the public. IPOs allow companies to raise capital from public investors.

- **Interest Rate:** The cost of borrowing money, expressed as a percentage. Interest rates are influenced by the Federal Reserve, economic conditions, and supply and demand for credit.

• **Interest Rate Risk:** The risk that changes in interest rates will adversely affect the value of an investment, particularly bonds.

J

• **Junk Bond:** A high-yield bond issued by a company with a low credit rating (below investment grade). Junk bonds offer higher potential returns but carry a significantly higher risk of default (the issuer failing to repay the bond).

L

• **Liquidity:** The ease with which an asset can be converted into cash without significant loss of value. Cash is the most liquid asset, while real estate, for example, is considered less liquid.

• **Long Position:** Owning an asset (stock, bond, etc.) with the expectation that its price will increase. Traders take long positions when they are bullish on a particular asset.

M

• **Market Capitalization (Market Cap):** The total dollar value of a company's outstanding shares of stock. Market cap is calculated by multiplying the current stock price by the number of outstanding shares. Companies are often categorized by market cap (large-cap, mid-cap, small-cap).

• **Market Index:** A statistical measure designed to track the performance of a specific segment of the stock market. Examples include the S&P 500, the Dow Jones Industrial Average, and the NASDAQ Composite.

• **Maturity Date:** The date on which a debt obligation, such as a bond, becomes due and payable. On the maturity date, the bond issuer repays the principal amount to the bondholder.

• **Money Market**: The market for short-term debt instruments (maturing in less than one year), such as Treasury bills, commercial paper, and certificates of deposit (CDs). The money market is highly liquid and considered relatively low-risk.

• **Mutual Fund**: A pool of money from many investors that is invested in a diversified portfolio of securities (stocks, bonds, or a combination). Mutual funds are managed by professional fund managers.

N

• **NASDAQ:** An electronic stock exchange that specializes in technology and growth companies. Many tech companies choose to list their shares on the NASDAQ.

O

• **Options:** Contracts that give the buyer the *right*, but not the *obligation*, to buy (call option) or sell (put option) an underlying asset (stock, index, etc.) at a specific price (strike price) on or before a specific date (expiration date). Options are derivative instruments.

P

- **Portfolio:** A collection of investments (stocks, bonds, mutual funds, real estate, etc.) owned by an individual or institution. A well-diversified portfolio is a key element of sound investment management.

- **Portfolio Diversification:** The strategy of spreading investments across different asset classes, sectors, and geographic regions to reduce overall portfolio risk.

- **Price-to-Earnings (P/E) Ratio**: A valuation ratio that compares a company's stock price to its earnings per share (EPS). The P/E ratio indicates how much investors are willing to pay for each dollar of a company's earnings. A high P/E ratio may suggest that investors have high expectations for future growth.

R

- **Real Estate:** Land and any structures built on it. Real estate can be a good long-term investment, offering both rental income and potential appreciation in value.

- **Risk Aversion**: The reluctance of an investor to take on investment risk. Risk-averse investors typically prefer lower-risk investments, such as bonds or money market funds.

S

- **S&P 500:** A market-capitalization-weighted index of 500 of the largest publicly traded companies in the United States. The S&P 500 is widely used as a benchmark to measure the overall performance of the U.S. stock market.

- **Securities and Exchange Commission (SEC):** The U.S. government agency responsible for regulating the securities markets and protecting investors.

- **Short Selling:** Borrowing securities (typically from a brokerage firm) and selling them with the expectation that the price will decline. If the price does decline, the short seller buys back the shares at the lower price and returns them to the lender, profiting from the difference. Short selling is a high-risk strategy.

T

- **Treasury Bills (T-Bills):** Short-term debt obligations issued by the U.S. government. T-bills are considered very low-risk investments.

V

- **Value Stock**: A stock of a company that appears to be undervalued relative to its fundamentals (earnings, assets, etc.). Value investors look for companies that are trading at a discount to their intrinsic value.

- **Volatility:** The degree of variation in the price of a security or the market as a whole. High volatility indicates that the price of an asset can fluctuate significantly, while low volatility suggests more stable prices.

W

• **Weighted Average Cost of Capital (WACC):** The average cost of all the capital a company has raised, including debt and equity. WACC is used to evaluate the profitability of a company's investments.

Y

• **Yield:** The income return on an investment, such as dividends from stocks or interest payments from bonds. Yield is typically expressed as a percentage of the investment's current price.

• **Yield Curve:** A graphical representation of the relationship between the interest rates and maturities of bonds (typically U.S. Treasury securities). The yield curve can provide insights into future economic conditions.

P (Continued)

• **Penny Stock:** A low-priced stock, typically trading for less than $5 per share. Penny stocks are highly speculative and carry significant risk.

• **Portfolio Rebalancing:** Periodically adjusting the asset allocation of a portfolio to maintain the desired level of risk and return.

• **Profit Target:** The price at which a trader plans to sell a security to realize a profit.

R (Continued)

• **Relative Strength Index (RSI):** A momentum indicator used to measure the speed and change of price movements.

• **Return on Investment (ROI):** A measure of the profitability of an investment, expressed as a percentage.

• **Risk:** The possibility of losing money on an investment.

S (Continued)

• **Sector:** A group of companies that operate in the same industry or related industries. Examples include the technology sector, the healthcare sector, and the energy sector.

• **Sell Limit Order:** An order to sell a security at or above a specified price.

• **Sell Stop Order:** An order to sell a security at or below a specified price.

• **Stop-Loss Order:** An order to sell a security when it reaches a certain price, designed to limit potential losses.

- **Swing Trading:** A trading strategy that involves holding securities for a few days or weeks, aiming to profit from short-term price swings.

T (Continued)

- **Technical Analysis:** A method of evaluating securities by studying historical price charts and trading volume data.

- **Ticker Symbol:** A unique abbreviation used to identify a publicly traded company's stock.

V (Continued)

- **Volume:** The number of shares of a security that are traded during a specific period.

- **(expiration date)**. Options are derivative instruments.

This list of financial terms provides a foundational vocabulary for navigating the world of investing and personal finance. While this is just a starting point, it's crucial to remember that continuous learning is essential for making informed financial decisions. Explore further, delve deeper into these concepts, and don't hesitate to seek guidance from qualified professionals. By expanding your knowledge and understanding of these terms and the underlying principles, you can empower yourself to make sound financial choices, build a strong financial future, and achieve your long-term financial goals.

Chapter 8: Understanding the Trading Landscape: Styles, Strategies, and the Trader's Mindset

This chapter provides a comprehensive overview of trading, exploring different trading styles, outlining the essential skills and psychological attributes of successful traders, and emphasizing the importance of a well-defined trading plan.

What is Trading? Capitalizing on Market Dynamics

Trading is the active pursuit of profit from short-term price fluctuations in financial markets. Unlike long-term investing, which focuses on holding assets for extended periods, trading involves frequent buying and selling of securities to capitalize on market movements. Traders aim to identify and exploit these price swings, whether they are driven by technical factors (chart patterns, indicators), fundamental news (earnings reports, economic data), or market sentiment. Trading requires a different skillset and mindset than investing, emphasizing speed, agility, and the ability to manage risk effectively. Traders utilize various tools and resources, including stock exchanges (NYSE, Nasdaq), online brokerage platforms, charting software, technical analysis indicators, and news feeds.

Trading Styles: Finding Your Fit

Different trading styles cater to different personalities, risk tolerances, and time commitments. Here's a breakdown of some common trading styles:

Day Trading: Day traders are the financial market equivalent of a sprint. Unlike long-term investors who patiently wait for their investments to mature, day traders are in a constant state of action, buying and selling securities *within the same trading day*. Every position is closed before the market's closing bell, ensuring no overnight exposure to market fluctuations. This rapid-fire trading style, while potentially lucrative, is not for the faint of heart.

The attraction of day trading is the potential for quick profits. Imagine capturing multiple small gains throughout the day, compounding them into substantial returns. This potential for rapid wealth creation is what draws many to this high-octane world. However, this potential reward comes at a steep price: *extremely high risk*.

Day trading is arguably the riskiest form of trading. The market can move against you in the blink of an eye, and a single bad trade can wipe out a significant portion of your capital. Because you're making multiple trades throughout the day, the commissions can also eat into your profits if you're not careful. The constant pressure and the rapid pace of trading can also take a toll on your mental and emotional well-being.

The Day Trader's Toolkit:

Successful day trading requires a unique combination of skills and knowledge:

- **Deep Understanding of Market Mechanics:** Day traders need a thorough understanding of how markets work, including order types, liquidity, bid-ask spreads, and the factors that drive price movements.

- **Mastery of Technical Analysis:** Technical analysis is the cornerstone of day trading. Day traders rely on charts, indicators, and patterns to identify short-term trading opportunities. They need to be able to quickly interpret price action and make informed decisions based on their analysis.

- **Rigorous Risk Management:** Risk management is paramount in day trading. Day traders must be able to define their risk tolerance, set stop-loss orders to limit potential losses, and manage their position size appropriately. They must also be prepared to accept losses quickly and move on to the next opportunity.

- **Emotional Discipline:** Emotions like fear and greed can be particularly detrimental to day traders. The fast-paced nature of day trading can amplify these emotions, leading to impulsive decisions and costly mistakes. Successful day traders must have the emotional discipline to stick to their trading plan and avoid letting emotions influence their decisions.

- **Access to the Right Tools and Technology:** Day trading requires access to fast and reliable trading platforms, real-time market data, and advanced charting software. Any lag or technical glitch can result in missed opportunities or significant losses.

A Day in the Life (and the Importance of a Plan):

Imagine a day trader's setup: multiple monitors displaying charts, news feeds, and order books. The trader is focused, analyzing price action, looking for patterns, and waiting for the right opportunity. They have a pre-defined trading plan, outlining their entry and exit criteria, risk tolerance, and profit targets. When a trade meets their criteria, they execute it quickly and decisively. They monitor the trade closely, ready to exit if it moves against them. At the end of the day, all positions are closed, and the trader reviews their performance, looking for areas for improvement.

Day trading is *not* a get-rich-quick scheme. It's a demanding profession that requires dedication, discipline, and a significant investment of time and effort. It's also highly risky and not suitable for beginners. Before venturing into the world of day trading, it's crucial to educate yourself thoroughly, practice on a demo account, and understand the risks involved. Many aspiring day traders lose their capital quickly due to a lack of preparation and understanding.

Day trading is a high-risk, high-reward endeavor that demands specialized skills, rigorous risk management, and emotional discipline. While the potential for quick profits is alluring, it's essential to approach day trading with caution and a realistic understanding of the challenges involved. It's not for everyone, and it's certainly not for beginners. Only those who are willing to dedicate the time and effort required to master the craft should consider day trading as a career.

Next we will take a look at swing trading.

Swing trading occupies a middle ground between the rapid-fire action of day trading and the long-term horizon of investing. Imagine a surfer who's not focused on the immediate thrill of each small wave like a day trader, nor waiting for the distant giant swell like an investor, but rather skillfully riding the medium-sized waves that offer a balance of excitement and a longer, more satisfying ride. That's the essence of swing trading: capturing the short-to-medium-term price swings in the market, holding positions for a few days to a few weeks, and profiting from the "swings" in price.

Swing trading requires a blend of both technical and fundamental analysis. Unlike day traders who primarily rely on technical charts, swing traders also consider the underlying fundamentals of a company. They look for companies with solid earnings, strong growth potential, or positive news catalysts that could drive a price swing. However, unlike long-term investors, they're not necessarily looking for deep value or long-term growth. They're more interested in identifying stocks that are likely to experience a short-to-medium-term price swing, regardless of their long-term prospects.

Momentum and Breakouts:

Swing traders are particularly interested in stocks that are exhibiting *momentum*. This means the stock price is moving strongly in a particular direction, either up or down. They also look for stocks that are showing signs of a potential *breakout* (moving above a key resistance level) or a *reversal* (changing direction from a downtrend to an uptrend, or vice versa). These breakouts and reversals can signal the start of a new price swing, providing opportunities for profit.

The Swing Trader's Toolkit:

Swing traders use a variety of tools and techniques to identify and capitalize on these price swings:

- **Technical Indicators:** Swing traders rely heavily on technical indicators to identify momentum, overbought/oversold conditions, and potential entry and exit points. Some commonly used indicators include moving averages, relative strength index (RSI), MACD, and volume indicators.

- **Chart Patterns:** Swing traders also look for chart patterns, such as triangles, flags, and head and shoulders patterns, which can provide clues about future price movements.

- **Fundamental Analysis:** While not as in-depth as a value investor, swing traders still consider fundamental factors like earnings reports, news events, and industry trends to assess the potential for a price swing.

- **Risk Management:** Risk management is crucial for swing trading. Swing traders must define their risk tolerance, set stop-loss orders to limit potential losses, and manage their position size appropriately. They must also be prepared to exit a trade if it's not working out as planned.

A Typical Swing Trade:

Imagine a swing trader who has identified a stock that's been consolidating in a tight range for several weeks. They notice that the stock's moving averages are starting to converge, and the RSI is showing signs of bullish divergence. They also see that the company is about to announce its earnings, and they believe the earnings report will be positive. Based on this analysis, the swing trader decides to enter a long position, anticipating a breakout above the resistance level. They set a stop-loss order below the resistance level to limit their potential losses.

A few days later, the company announces better-than-expected earnings, and the stock price surges, breaking out above the resistance level. The swing trader monitors the trade closely, waiting for the price to reach their target profit level. After a few more days, the stock price reaches the target, and the swing trader closes the position, locking in their profit.

The Advantages of Swing Trading:

- **Less Time-Consuming than Day Trading:** Swing trading doesn't require the constant monitoring and split-second decision-making of day trading. Traders can typically manage their positions with a few hours of analysis each day.

- **Potential for Larger Profits than Day Trading:** Because swing trades last longer than day trades, the potential for profit is generally greater.

- **More Flexibility than Long-Term Investing:** Swing trading offers more flexibility than long-term investing, allowing traders to capitalize on shorter-term market movements.

The Challenges of Swing Trading:

- **Requires a Combination of Skills:** Swing trading requires a balance of technical and fundamental analysis, as well as risk management skills.

- **Can Be Emotionally Challenging:** Swing traders must be able to manage their emotions and avoid letting fear or greed influence their decisions.

- **Requires Patience:** Swing trades can take several days or weeks to play out, requiring patience and discipline.

Swing trading offers a compelling middle ground for traders seeking to capitalize on short-to-medium-term market movements. It requires a blend of technical and fundamental analysis, a focus on momentum and breakouts, and a disciplined approach to risk management. While it's less time-consuming than day trading, it still demands dedication, education, and a thorough understanding of market dynamics. For those who are willing to put in the effort, swing trading can be a rewarding and profitable pursuit.

Next we have position trading.

Position trading is the marathon runner of the trading world. Unlike the sprinters of day trading or the middle-distance runners of swing trading, position traders are in it for the long haul. They hold positions for weeks, months, or even years, focusing on capturing the major, long-term trends in the market. Think of a seasoned sailor, charting a course across vast oceans, less concerned with the choppy waves of the day and more focused on the prevailing winds and currents that will guide them to their destination. That's the essence of position trading: capitalizing on the *big picture*, the overarching market trends, rather than getting caught up in the daily noise.

The Primacy of Fundamental Analysis:

Position trading is fundamentally driven. While technical analysis can play a supporting role in identifying entry and exit points, the primary focus is on the *intrinsic value* of the asset. Position traders meticulously analyze company financials, industry trends, economic data, and global events to identify opportunities with long-term growth potential. They seek companies with strong fundamentals: solid earnings, healthy balance sheets, innovative products or services, and capable management teams. They're looking for companies they believe will thrive over the long term, regardless of short-term market fluctuations.

Ignoring the Daily Noise:

One of the hallmarks of position trading is its disregard for short-term price swings. Position traders understand that the market can be volatile in the short term, influenced by news events, sentiment shifts, and even algorithmic trading. They accept these fluctuations as part of the market's natural rhythm and don't let them shake their conviction in their long-term analysis. They're focused on the *forest*, not the individual trees.

The Position Trader's Mindset:

Successful position trading requires a unique set of characteristics:

- **Patience:** Position trades can take weeks or months to play out. Traders must have the patience to wait for their investment thesis to materialize, without being tempted to exit prematurely due to short-term market volatility.

- **Long-Term Vision:** Position traders need a long-term perspective. They're not looking for quick profits; they're looking for investments that will appreciate significantly over time.

- **Conviction:** Position traders must have strong conviction in their fundamental analysis. They need to be able to stick to their investment thesis even when the market is moving against them.

- **Emotional Discipline:** While less prone to the emotional rollercoaster of short-term trading, position traders still need emotional discipline. They must be able to resist the urge to panic sell during market downturns and avoid getting caught up in market hype.

- **Thorough Research:** Position trading requires in-depth research and due diligence. Traders must be able to analyze financial statements, understand industry dynamics, and assess the long-term prospects of a company.

A Position Trade Example:

Imagine a position trader who has identified a growing trend in renewable energy. They research several companies in the solar industry and identify one with strong financials, innovative technology, and a solid management team. They believe that the demand for solar energy will continue to increase over the next several years, and they anticipate that this company will be a major beneficiary of this trend. They decide to take a long position in the company's stock, with a time horizon of several years.

Over the next few months, the stock price fluctuates, sometimes moving against the position trader. However, they remain confident in their long-term analysis and don't let these short-term fluctuations deter them. Eventually, their thesis plays out, and the stock price appreciates significantly as the demand for solar energy increases.

The Advantages of Position Trading:

- **Less Time-Consuming:** Position trading requires less time and attention than day trading or swing trading. Traders can typically manage their positions with a few hours of research and analysis per week.

- **Potential for Larger Gains:** By capturing long-term market trends, position traders have the potential for larger gains than short-term traders.

- **Lower Trading Costs:** Because they trade less frequently, position traders incur lower trading costs.

The Challenges of Position Trading:

- **Requires Patience and Discipline:** Position trading requires patience and the ability to resist short-term market pressures.

- **Requires Thorough Research:** Successful position trading requires in-depth fundamental analysis.

- **Can Be Subject to Unexpected Events:** Long-term investments can be affected by unexpected events, such as economic downturns or changes in industry dynamics.

Position trading is a long-term investment strategy that focuses on capturing major market trends. It requires a deep understanding of fundamental analysis, a long-term vision, and the ability to ignore short-term market noise. While it demands patience and discipline, it can be a rewarding approach for investors seeking long-term growth and less concerned with the daily fluctuations of the market.

Scalping on the other hand, is the financial market equivalent of a hummingbird flitting from flower to flower, gathering tiny sips of nectar from each. It's the most extreme form of short-term trading, where positions are held for mere seconds to minutes, sometimes even less. Scalpers aim to profit from the smallest price fluctuations, the tiny ticks and micro-movements that most traders wouldn't even notice. It's a high-octane, high-pressure world where speed and precision are paramount.

Scalpers aren't looking for big wins. They're after numerous small profits, which they accumulate throughout the trading day. The idea is that these small gains, when added together, can generate substantial returns over time. It's a game of volume and frequency, where the sheer number of trades executed is as important as the size of each individual profit.

Lightning-Fast Execution:

Scalping demands lightning-fast execution. Scalpers need to be able to enter and exit trades in the blink of an eye, reacting instantly to changing market conditions. Any hesitation or delay can mean the difference between a small profit and a missed opportunity, or even a small loss. This requires access to high-speed trading platforms, real-time market data, and a deep understanding of order types and market mechanics.

The Scalper's Skillset:

Successful scalping requires a very specific skill set:

- **Exceptional Speed and Reflexes:** Scalpers need to be able to react quickly to market movements, executing trades with speed and precision.

- **Mastery of Level 2 Data:** Level 2 data provides real-time insights into the order book, showing the bid and ask prices, as well as the size of the orders waiting to be filled. This information is crucial for scalpers to identify short-term trading opportunities.

- **Deep Understanding of Market Microstructure:** Scalpers need to understand the intricacies of market microstructure, including how orders are routed, how liquidity works, and how market makers operate.

- **Rigorous Risk Management:** While individual losses on each trade are small, the sheer volume of trades executed by scalpers means that risk management is absolutely essential. A string of small losses can quickly add up to a significant drawdown. Scalpers must be disciplined in setting stop-loss orders and managing their position size.

- **Mental Fortitude:** Scalping is an incredibly stressful and demanding activity. The constant pressure to make quick decisions, the rapid-fire trading environment, and the potential for losses can take a toll on even the most experienced traders. Scalpers need to have exceptional mental fortitude and the ability to manage stress effectively.

Some people may disagree with me but I feel scalping should generally not be recommended for beginners for several reasons:

- **Steep Learning Curve:** Mastering the skills and knowledge required for successful scalping takes time and effort. Beginners are likely to lose money quickly if they attempt to scalp without proper preparation.

- **High Risk:** The fast-paced nature of scalping and the sheer volume of trades executed make it extremely risky, especially for those who are new to trading.

- **Emotional Toll:** The stress and pressure of scalping can be overwhelming for beginners, leading to poor decision-making and emotional burnout.

- **Requires Specialized Tools and Technology:** Scalping requires access to expensive trading platforms, real-time data feeds, and other specialized tools that can be costly for beginners.

A Normal Scalping Scenario:

A scalper is watching Level 2 data for a particular stock. They notice a large buy order coming in, indicating strong buying pressure. They quickly enter a long position, anticipating a small price increase. Within seconds, the price ticks up a few cents, and the scalper exits the position, locking in their small profit. They repeat this process hundreds of times throughout the day, accumulating small profits from each trade.

Scalping is a highly specialized and demanding trading style that's not for everyone. It requires exceptional speed, deep market knowledge, rigorous risk management, and strong mental fortitude. While the potential for quick profits is alluring, the risks are equally high. Beginners are strongly advised to avoid scalping until they have gained significant experience and knowledge in other trading styles. It's a world for seasoned professionals, not for those just starting their trading journey.

From Sports Cards to Stocks: A Foundation in Market Principles

My early fascination with collecting sports cards provided a valuable, albeit unconscious, introduction to the principles of market trading. Analyzing player performance, anticipating demand, and negotiating trades for coveted cards instilled in me a basic understanding of supply and demand, valuation, and negotiation – all skills that are directly applicable to the stock market. This early experience sparked my interest in the financial markets and laid the foundation for my trading journey.

The Importance of a Trading Plan: Your Roadmap to Success

A well-defined trading plan is absolutely essential for success in trading. It serves as your roadmap, guiding your decisions and keeping you focused on your goals. A trading plan should include:

- **Trading Strategy:** A clear description of your trading style, the types of securities you will trade, and the methods you will use to identify trading opportunities.
- **Risk Tolerance:** Your willingness to accept losses.
- **Money Management Rules:** Guidelines for position sizing, stop-loss orders, and overall capital allocation.
- **Entry and Exit Rules:** Specific criteria for entering and exiting trades.
- **Record Keeping:** A system for tracking your trades and analyzing your performance.

We will delve into the details of creating a comprehensive trading plan in a later chapter.

Challenge of the Market: A Vast and Dynamic Landscape

The financial markets are a vast and dynamic landscape, a colossal engine of capital flowing through an intricate network of exchanges, algorithms, and human decisions. As an individual trader, it's easy to feel like a small player in this immense arena. But even small-time traders can find their niche, develop a winning strategy, and achieve their financial goals. The key is to approach trading with a combination of knowledge, discipline, patience, and a well-defined plan

Chapter 9: Finding Your Edge: Turning Personal Experience into Market Insights

The stock market, a vast and dynamic ecosystem teeming with opportunities and challenges, can often feel overwhelming. It's easy to get lost in the sea of data, complex jargon, and ever-shifting trends. Many aspiring traders believe that only seasoned professionals with advanced degrees and insider connections can truly succeed. However, a powerful and often overlooked resource lies within each of us: our personal experiences. This chapter explores how you can leverage your unique background, knowledge, and everyday observations to develop a distinctive edge in the market, turning seemingly ordinary life experiences into valuable investment insights. It's about defining your niche, your unique advantage in the trading world.

The Illusion of Complexity: Demystifying the Market

The financial markets often appear shrouded in mystery, intentionally or unintentionally. Financial institutions, analysts, and commentators sometimes use complex terminology and convoluted explanations that can intimidate and discourage new traders. However, beneath the surface, the fundamental principles of investing and trading are often quite simple. At its core, it's about understanding businesses, identifying trends, and making informed decisions based on your insights and analysis. You don't need a PhD in finance to do this. In fact, sometimes, a fresh perspective, unburdened by conventional wisdom and Wall Street jargon, can be a significant advantage.

Your Unique Advantage: Turning Life Experience into Market Insights

Think about your daily life. What products do you use? What services do you rely on? What industries are you familiar with? What are your passions and hobbies? These seemingly mundane aspects of your life can provide valuable clues about market trends and potential investment opportunities.

- **Consumer Trends:** Are you noticing a particular brand becoming increasingly popular among your friends or colleagues? Are there new technologies emerging that are changing the way people live, work, or interact with the world? These observations can provide valuable insights into which companies are likely to thrive in the future. For example, if you see a surge in popularity for plant-based foods in your social circle and local grocery stores, you might consider researching companies that produce or distribute these products. Or, if you notice that more and more people are using voice assistants like Alexa or Siri, you might explore investment opportunities in companies involved in artificial intelligence and natural language processing.

- **Industry Knowledge:** If you work in a particular industry, you have firsthand knowledge of its dynamics, challenges, and opportunities. This insider perspective can be invaluable for identifying promising investments within that industry. For instance, if you work in the healthcare industry, you might be aware of new medical devices, treatments, or pharmaceutical drugs that are showing promising results in clinical trials. This knowledge could lead you to invest in companies developing these innovations before they become widely known to the public.

- **Personal Experiences:** Even your hobbies and interests can spark investment ideas. If you're an avid gamer, you might be keenly aware of the latest trends in gaming, the most popular games, and the companies developing cutting-edge gaming hardware and software. This passion could translate into a deep understanding of the gaming industry and its key players, giving you an edge when evaluating gaming stocks. Similarly, if you're a fitness enthusiast, you might be attuned to the latest trends in fitness equipment, athletic wear, and health supplements, potentially leading you to identify promising investment opportunities in those areas.

Examples of Everyday Insights: From Coffee to Cloud Computing

Let's look at some concrete examples of how everyday experiences can be transformed into investment ideas:

- **The Coffee Shop Phenomenon:** Have you noticed an increasing number of specialty coffee shops popping up in your neighborhood? This trend could indicate a growing demand for high-quality coffee and unique coffee experiences, potentially making coffee chains, coffee roasters, or related businesses attractive investment opportunities.

- **The Rise of Streaming Entertainment:** The ongoing shift from traditional cable TV to streaming services is a clear trend that has created enormous opportunities for companies like Netflix, Disney+, and Amazon Prime Video. Recognizing this trend early on and investing in these companies could have led to significant gains.

- **The Cloud Computing Revolution:** The increasing reliance on cloud computing is transforming the way businesses operate and store data. Understanding this trend could lead you to invest in companies like Amazon Web Services (AWS), Microsoft Azure, or Google Cloud Platform, which are major players in the cloud computing market.

Developing Your Edge: Research and Due Diligence

Once you've identified a potential investment idea based on your personal experiences or observations, it's crucial to conduct thorough research and due diligence. Don't rely solely on your gut feeling or initial impression. Dig deeper. Learn as much as you can about the company, its competitors, its industry, and its financial performance. Read financial news articles, analyze the company's financial statements (balance sheet, income statement, cash flow statement), and consult with financial advisors if necessary.

Developing an edge in the market requires cultivating a "trader's mindset." This means being observant, curious, and always on the lookout for patterns, trends, and anomalies. Pay close attention to the world around you, ask questions, and consider how these observations might translate into investment opportunities. Develop a habit of connecting the dots between seemingly unrelated events and trends. Developing an edge in the market requires more than just technical skills; it requires cultivating a specific mindset. A "trader's mindset" is characterized by:

- **Curiosity:** Successful traders are naturally curious and constantly seeking to understand how the world works. They ask questions, challenge assumptions, and are always eager to learn.

- **Observational Skills:** Pay close attention to the world around you. Observe patterns, trends, and anomalies in consumer behavior, technology, and other areas that could translate into investment opportunities.

- **Skepticism:** Don't take everything at face value. Be skeptical of hype and always do your own research. Challenge conventional wisdom and look for evidence to support or refute claims.

- **Adaptability:** The market is constantly changing. Be prepared to adapt your strategies and adjust your thinking as new information becomes available.

Practical Steps:

- **Read Widely:** Read financial news, industry publications, company reports, and books on investing and trading.
- **Follow Industry Leaders:** Stay informed about the views and insights of respected investors and analysts.
- **Network with Other Traders:** Share ideas and learn from the experiences of other traders.
- **Develop a Research Process:** Create a systematic approach to conducting due diligence. This will help you stay organized and ensure that you're covering all the important areas.
- **Practice:** The more you practice your research and analysis skills, the better you'll become at identifying promising investment opportunities.

By combining thorough research and due diligence with a curious, observant, and adaptable mindset, you can develop a true edge in the market and significantly improve your chances of success.

Combining Personal Insights with Market Knowledge

The most successful investors and traders combine their personal insights with a deep understanding of market principles and analytical tools. They don't just rely on intuition or gut feelings; they back up their hunches with solid research, analysis, and risk management. By combining your unique perspective with sound investment principles, you can create a powerful edge in the market.

Decoding Everyday Trends: The Consumer as a Guide

Our experiences as consumers provide a constant stream of valuable data. Pay attention to the products and services that are gaining popularity, the emerging trends, and the companies that are innovating and disrupting their industries. Are you seeing a particular brand of clothing or footwear becoming increasingly popular among your friends and social media influencers? Are there new restaurants or cafes opening up that are consistently packed with customers? These real-world observations can be valuable indicators of a company's potential success. While anecdotal evidence alone isn't enough to base investment decisions on, it can serve as a valuable starting point for further research. Your personal experiences can help you identify potential investment opportunities before they become widely recognized by the market.

The Insider's Perspective: Leveraging Industry Knowledge

If you work in a specific industry, you have access to a wealth of information that is not readily available to the general public. You might be aware of upcoming product launches, changes in management, shifts in market dynamics, or emerging trends within your industry. This insider perspective can be incredibly valuable when evaluating companies in your field. However, it's crucial to be mindful of insider trading regulations and ensure that you only use publicly available information when making investment decisions. Your industry knowledge can help you interpret market signals, identify potential risks and opportunities, and potentially uncover undervalued companies.

Turning Hobbies into Investments: Passion Meets Profit

Our hobbies and passions can also be a source of valuable investment insights. If you're a car enthusiast, you might be closely following the latest developments in the automotive industry, including the rise of electric vehicles, autonomous driving technology, or the emergence of new mobility solutions. This passion can translate into a deep understanding of the industry, its key players, and its future trajectory, giving you an edge when evaluating automotive stocks. Similarly, if you're a passionate foodie, you might be aware of the latest culinary trends, the success of up-and-coming restaurant chains, or the growing demand for sustainable and ethically sourced food. Your passion can fuel your research and lead you to identify promising investment opportunities that others might miss.

Beyond the Obvious: Connecting the Dots

Sometimes, the most valuable insights come from connecting seemingly unrelated dots and thinking critically about how broader trends might impact different industries and companies. Consider how changes in demographics, technology, social values, or geopolitical events might influence various sectors. For example, the rise of remote work has had a significant impact on the real estate market (demand for suburban homes), the technology sector (demand for video conferencing and collaboration tools), and even the demand for certain consumer goods (home office furniture, athleisure wear). By thinking critically about how these trends intersect and influence different sectors, you can identify investment opportunities that others might overlook.

Avoiding Emotional Bias: The Importance of Objectivity

While leveraging personal experiences and insights can be a powerful advantage, it's important to be aware of potential biases. Our personal preferences, experiences, and emotional attachments can sometimes cloud our judgment and lead us to make irrational investment decisions. For example, if you're a loyal customer of a particular brand, you might be overly optimistic about its future prospects, even if the company's fundamentals are deteriorating or its competitive landscape is shifting. It's crucial to remain objective, conduct thorough research, and avoid letting your emotions influence your investment decisions.

Chapter 10: Sheet Music.

You don't improvise on stage without a score; you don't enter the market without a plan.

Chart formations are invaluable tools in the arsenal of technical analysts. They represent recurring visual patterns in price action that can provide valuable insights into market sentiment and potential future price movements. These patterns, formed by the interplay of supply and demand, offer traders a visual roadmap of potential trading opportunities.

Recognizing and interpreting chart patterns requires careful observation, discipline, and a deep understanding of market psychology. By studying these formations, traders can anticipate potential price reversals, identify continuation trends, and make more informed entry and exit decisions.

Some common chart patterns include triangles, flags, pennants, head and shoulders, and double tops/bottoms. Each pattern has distinct characteristics and implications, suggesting potential price targets and stop-loss levels.

However, it's crucial to remember that chart patterns are not foolproof predictors. Market conditions are constantly evolving, and unexpected events can disrupt even the most promising patterns. Therefore, it's essential to use chart patterns in conjunction with other technical indicators and fundamental analysis for a more comprehensive trading strategy.

By diligently studying chart patterns and integrating them into your trading plan, you can gain a valuable edge in navigating the complexities of the financial markets.

When you search for a stock or ETF within your brokerage account, you'll often have the option to view candlestick charts. I find candlestick charts particularly valuable due to the wealth of information they provide. Each candlestick represents a specific time period, offering insights into price action within that time frame. By analyzing the patterns formed by these candlesticks, you can make more informed trading decisions.

While candlestick patterns can be powerful tools, it's crucial to remember that they are not foolproof predictors. No trading strategy guarantees 100% accuracy. By identifying and utilizing these patterns, you aim to increase your probability of success. A 50/50 chance of success is clearly less desirable than a 70/30 or higher probability. It is your job to find the patterns, setups and, assets that give YOU the best probability to win in the trade.

Below is an explanation on the information provided in 1 candlestick.

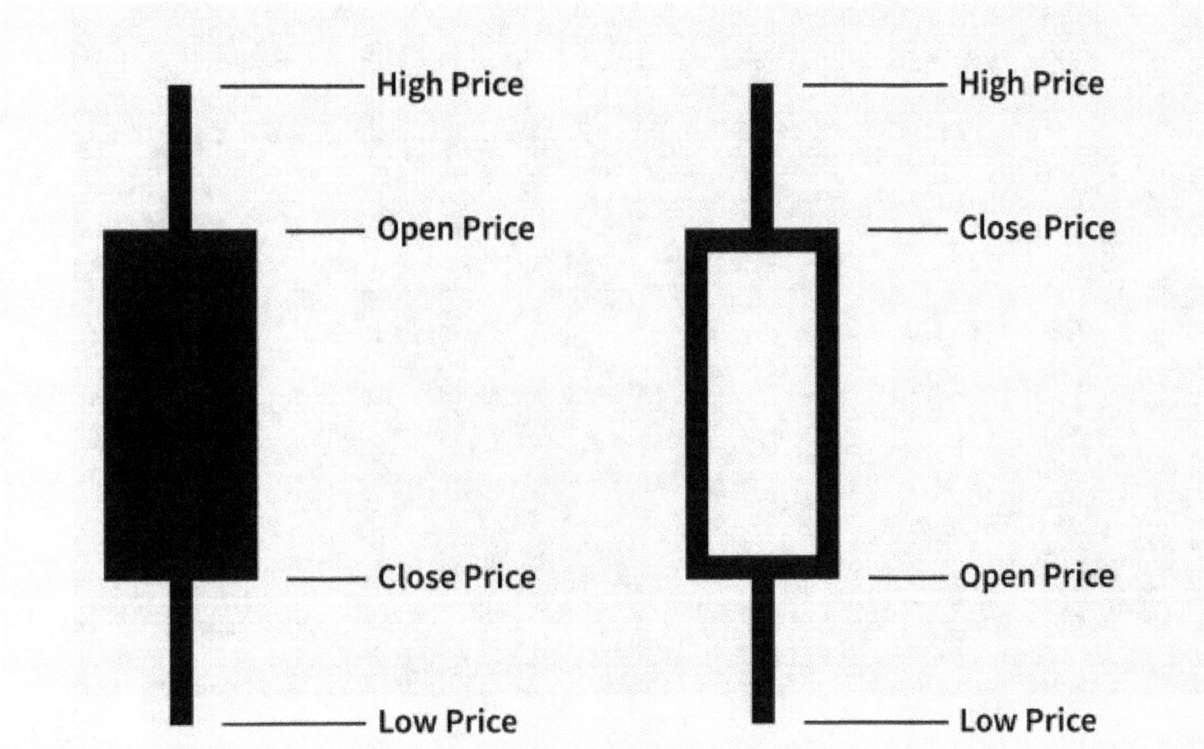

Imagine a candlestick chart as a captivating story unfolding before your very eyes. Each individual candlestick, a unique visual narrative, whispers tales of market sentiment, revealing the ebb and flow of supply and demand during a specific timeframe. These miniature masterpieces, with their distinct bodies and shadows, paint a vivid picture of the market's inner workings.

The beauty of candlestick charts lies in their versatility. Like a skilled conductor adjusting the tempo of an orchestra, you can seamlessly shift the time frame, zooming in and out to explore different rhythms and harmonies of price action. From the frenetic dance of intraday fluctuations, measured in seconds and minutes, to the grand, sweeping movements of yearly trends, each time frame offers a unique perspective on the market's character.

By meticulously studying these visual narratives, traders can decipher hidden patterns, anticipate potential turning points, and gain valuable insights into the market's psychology. Whether you're a seasoned veteran or a curious newcomer, the art of reading candlestick charts offers a fascinating window into the dynamic world of trading.

5 Year Chart with 1 week candles Charts Courtesy of Tradingview.com

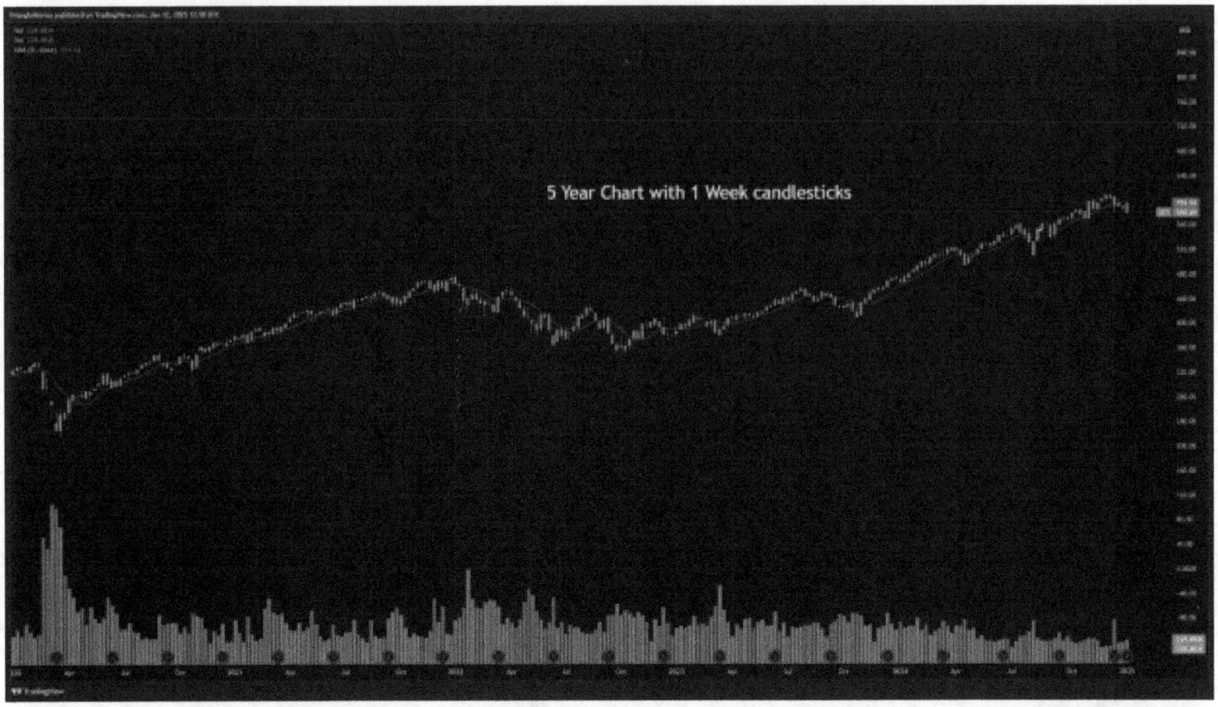

1 day chart with 1 minute candlesticks Charts Courtesy of Tradingview.com

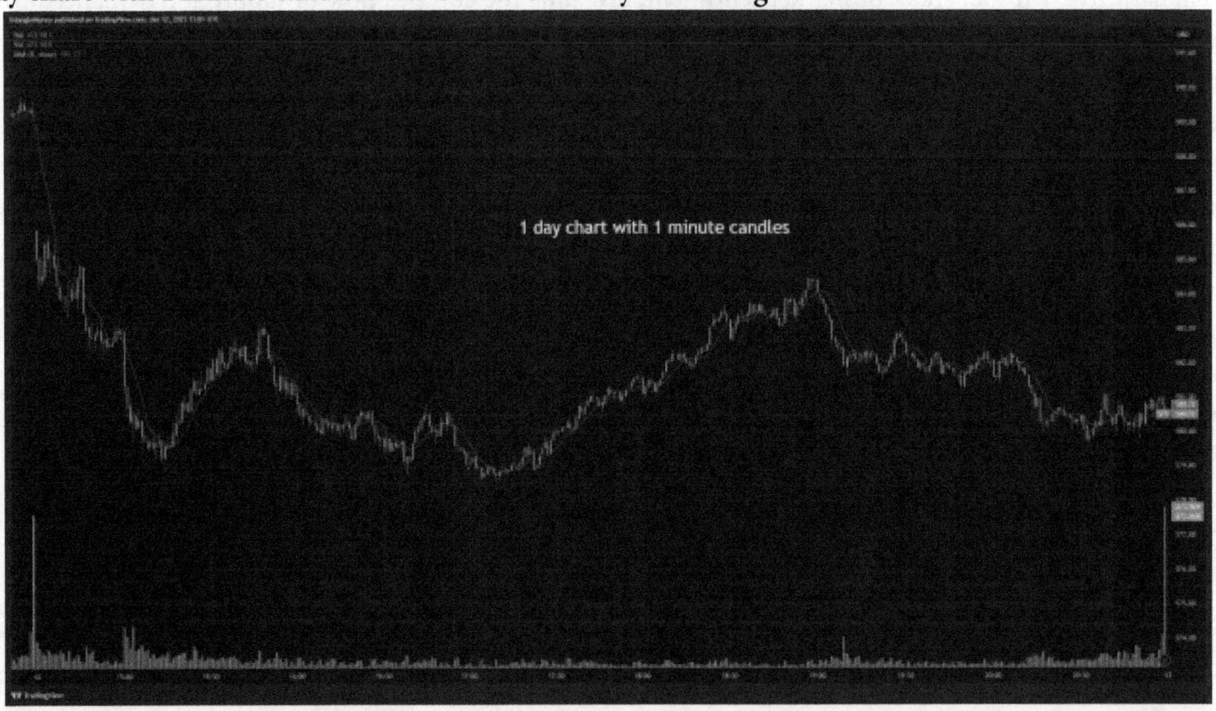

Determining your trading timeframe is crucial. How long will you hold a position? Will you be a day trader, a swing trader, or a long-term investor? This decision will significantly impact your trading strategy, risk tolerance, and the types of opportunities you pursue. Establishing clear entry and exit criteria, including profit targets and stop-loss orders, is essential for successful trading.

Powerful Tools for Informed Trading

Indicators are valuable tools that can enhance your trading decisions by providing additional insights into price movements and potential trading opportunities. However, it's important to avoid information overload. Select a few indicators that resonate with your trading style and complement your overall trading strategy. Three indicators that have proven effective for me are trend lines, volume analysis, and Fibonacci retracements. Ideally, I look for at least two of these indicators to align before entering a trade.

Patience

Discipline and patience are essential when using indicators. Don't chase trades that don't meet your criteria. Remember, it's better to miss a potential opportunity than enter a trade that doesn't align with your strategy. This disciplined approach helps minimize losses. At the end of the day it's not about how much money you make but how much you don't lose.

Market Cycles Explained
Infographic Courtesy of thetechnicaltrader.com Figure 1

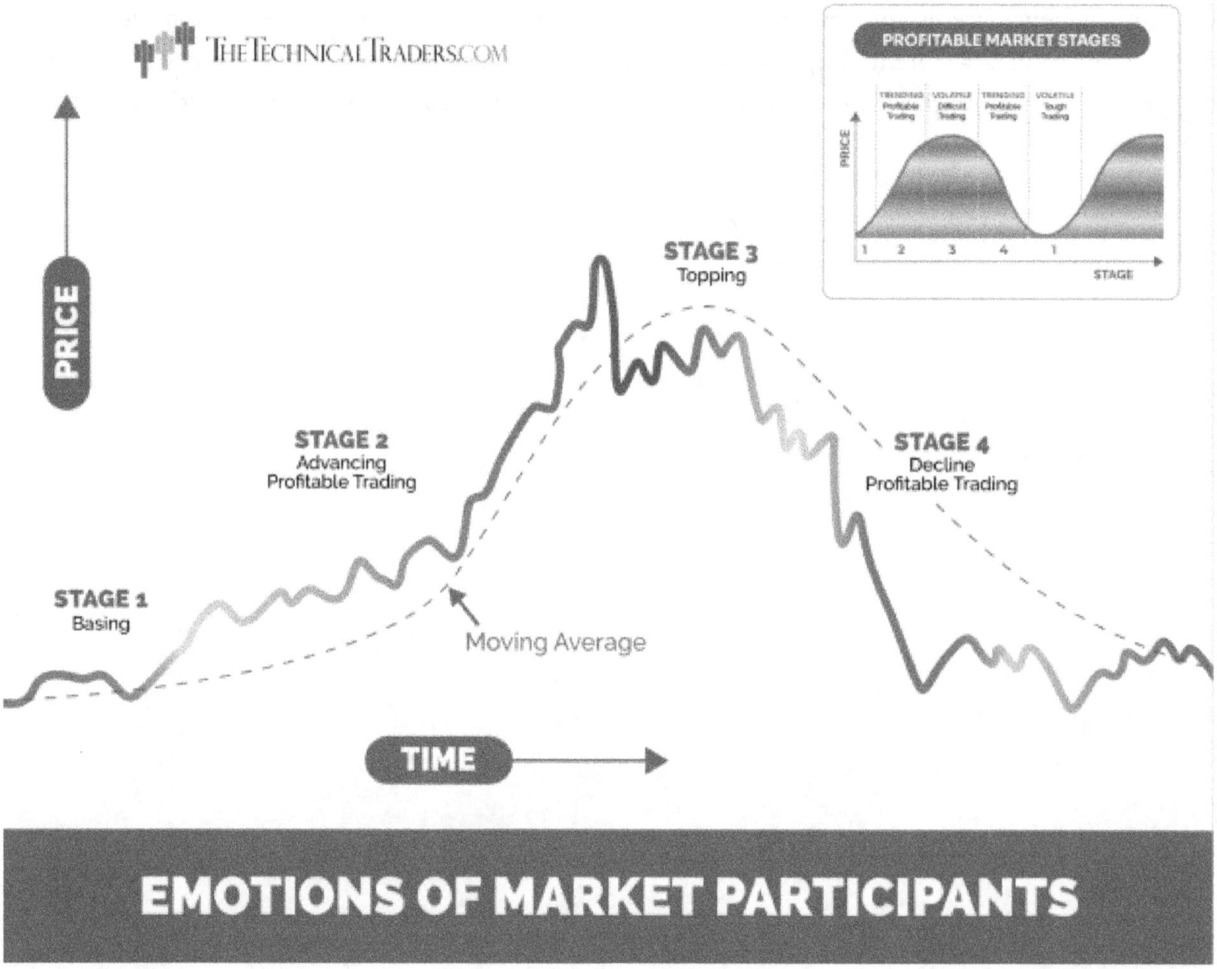

Timing entries and exits is the most crucial aspect of successful trading. The exit to me is more important. It speaks to how you will manage the position once you enter. Observe chart 1 in Stage 1, the basing stage. Notice how the price reaches the moving average and then begins to trend upward. This initial upward movement serves as my primary buy signal. I typically initiate a small position at this stage.

Once the upward trend is confirmed, as observed in Stage 2, I consider adding to my position. By the time the price reaches Stage 3, technical indicators should signal potential profit-taking opportunities.

A significant advantage of trading is the ability to profit from both rising and falling markets. You can employ various strategies to capitalize on both upward and downward price movements, including options and inverse ETFs.

Market Cycles Explained
Infographic Courtesy of thetechnicaltrader.com Figure 2

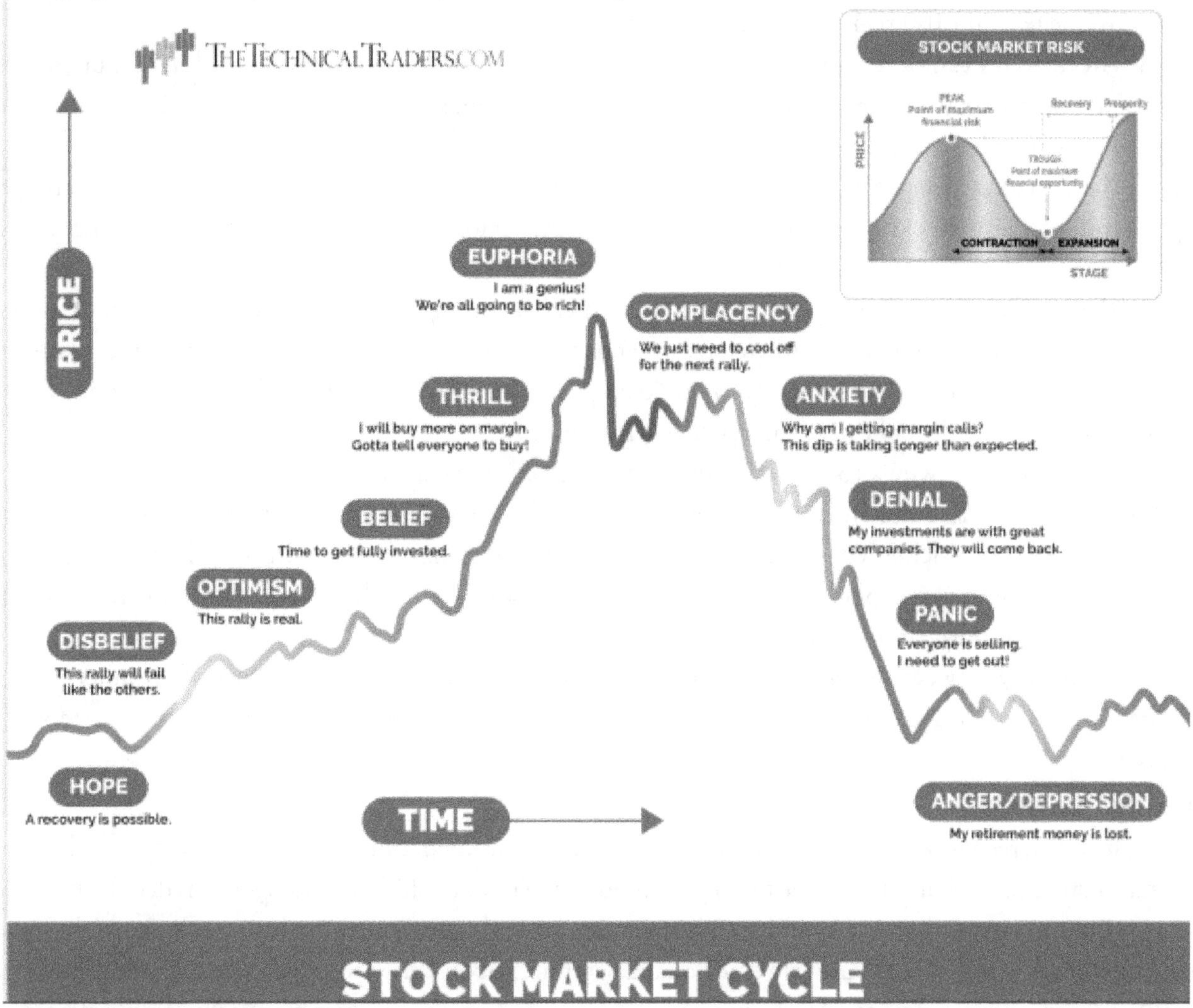

Chart 2 illustrates how emotions, primarily fear and greed, drive price movements in the markets. These emotions fuel volatility and trading volume. Unfortunately, many traders succumb to these emotions, buying at market tops when greed is rampant and selling at market bottoms when fear prevails.

To succeed, it's crucial to act counterintuitively. Buy when others are fearful and sell when others are greedy. However, consistently timing these market extremes requires a well-defined trading system and disciplined execution. Remember the adage: 'You can't catch a falling knife.' Attempting to time the absolute bottom of a market decline is often futile.

Patience and rigorous research are essential. Develop a robust trading plan and stick to it, allowing your research and analysis to guide your decisions, not your emotions.

Fear and Greed

The Fear & Greed Index, developed by CNN Business, is a tool designed to gauge the current emotional state of the stock market. It operates on the premise that investor emotions, such as fear and greed, significantly influence stock prices.

Essentially, the index attempts to quantify the degree of fear or greed prevailing in the market. High readings suggest excessive greed, potentially indicating overvalued stocks. Conversely, low readings signal significant fear, which could suggest that stocks are undervalued.

The index is calculated by analyzing seven different market indicators, such as stock price momentum, market volatility, and put/call option ratios. These indicators are then combined to produce a score on a scale of 0 to 100, with 0 representing extreme fear and 100 representing extreme greed.

The Fear & Greed Index can be a valuable tool for swing traders, although it should be used in conjunction with other technical and fundamental analysis. Swing traders aim to capitalize on short-term price fluctuations, often holding positions for a few days to a few weeks.

Imagine the stock market as a vast ballroom, where investors waltz to the ever-changing rhythms of fear and greed. These two powerful emotions, like the opposing forces of gravity and buoyancy, constantly tug at the market's delicate equilibrium.

Fear, the cautious whisper in the back of your mind, can quickly turn into a deafening roar. Whispers of recession, geopolitical tensions, or unforeseen black swan events can send shivers down investors' spines, triggering a stampede for the exits. Panic selling ensues, as traders scramble to liquidate positions, often at any price. The market, once buoyant, suddenly plummets, mirroring the collective anxiety that grips the crowd.

But fear, like a pendulum, swings to its opposite extreme: greed. Fueled by whispers of burgeoning economies, technological breakthroughs, and the intoxicating scent of easy profits, greed can ignite a speculative frenzy. Investors, blinded by the allure of quick riches, chase after the next hot stock, driving prices to dizzying heights. The market, intoxicated by optimism, enters a euphoric state, where valuations soar, logic takes a backseat, and the whispers of caution are drowned out by the clamor of exuberance.

This constant interplay between fear and greed creates a dynamic and unpredictable market environment. Bubbles inflate and burst, fortunes are made and lost, and the market, like a seasoned dancer, navigates the intricate steps of this emotional tango.

Mastering the Dance

For the avid investor, recognizing and understanding the profound influence of emotions on investment decisions is absolutely paramount. The stock market, while often presented as a realm of cold, calculated logic, is deeply intertwined with human psychology. Greed, fear, panic, and even overconfidence can significantly impact our choices, often leading to suboptimal outcomes. It's crucial to cultivate emotional discipline, to resist the seductive siren call of excessive greed and the paralyzing grip of irrational fear. Mastering one's emotions is arguably as important as understanding market mechanics.

Foundations of Sound Investing

Base all investment decisions on sound analysis, thorough fundamental research, and a well-defined, long-term perspective. Avoid impulsive reactions driven by market noise, fleeting trends, or emotional outbursts. Develop a clear investment strategy based on your individual financial goals, risk tolerance, and time horizon, and stick to it. Don't let short-term market fluctuations or the opinions of others sway you from your carefully considered plan. Rationality is the bedrock of successful investing, providing a stable foundation amidst the market's inherent volatility.

The Shield Against Uncertainty

Spread your investments across a diverse range of asset classes, sectors, and geographic regions to mitigate risk and reduce your exposure to market volatility. Diversification is not about maximizing returns in the short term; it's about protecting your capital and ensuring long-term stability. By diversifying, you reduce the impact of any single investment's poor performance on your overall portfolio. Think of it as building a portfolio that can withstand various market conditions, rather than one that is overly reliant on the success of a few select holdings. A well-diversified portfolio acts as a buffer against the unpredictable nature of the market.

Maintaining a Long-Term Perspective

Focus on your long-term investment goals and time horizon. Short-term market fluctuations, while often unsettling, should not derail your long-term investment strategy. The market is inherently cyclical, with periods of growth followed by inevitable corrections and even bear markets. Trying to time the market is notoriously difficult, even for professional investors. Instead of attempting to predict short-term movements, concentrate on building a portfolio that can grow steadily over time, weathering the inevitable ups and downs of the market cycle. A long-term perspective allows you to ride out the storms and reap the rewards of compounding growth.

Recognizing and Acknowledging Your Biases

We all harbor inherent biases, whether it's the fear of missing out (FOMO), the tendency to overestimate our ability to predict market movements (overconfidence bias), the anchoring bias (relying too heavily on the first piece of information received), or confirmation bias (seeking out information that confirms our existing beliefs). Acknowledging these biases is the crucial first step towards mitigating their influence on our investment decisions. Be aware of your emotional triggers and develop strategies to counteract them. Seek out diverse perspectives and challenge your own assumptions. By understanding our own psychological tendencies, we can make more objective and rational investment choices.

Cultivating Emotional Discipline: The Key to Long-Term Success

Ultimately, successful investing requires cultivating emotional discipline. This means developing the ability to remain calm and rational in the face of market volatility, to resist the temptation to chase short-term gains, and to stick to your long-term investment strategy even when others are panicking. It's about developing a mindset that prioritizes long-term growth over short-term gratification. By navigating the market's emotional currents with a calm and disciplined mind, investors can significantly increase their chances of weathering the inevitable storms, avoiding costly mistakes, and reaping the substantial rewards of long-term investment success. Emotional intelligence is just as important as financial intelligence when it comes to building and preserving wealth.

Chapter 11: A Beginner's Guide to Technical Indicators

Indicators fall into two broad categories: lagging and leading indicators.

- **Lagging Indicators:** These indicators confirm trends after they've already materialized. They are useful for identifying the overall trend direction but may not provide precise entry or exit points.

- **Leading Indicators:** These indicators attempt to predict future price movements, such as potential reversals. They often identify overbought or oversold conditions, suggesting potential price corrections. However, leading indicators are not foolproof, and their predictive accuracy can be limited.

The most effective approach to indicators is to experiment and discover what works best for you. Explore the various indicator types explained in the terms section of this book. Backtest your strategies using historical data to assess their effectiveness before risking real capital. Remember, indicators are tools to enhance your analysis, not a guaranteed path to success.

Indicator Class	Identifies
Trending Indicators	The direction of the current trend and also reversals
Momentum Indicators	Overbought and Oversold Levels
Volume Indicators	Increased Volume
Volatility Indicators	Increased Volatility

Moving Averages

Moving averages are fundamental tools in technical analysis, designed to smooth out price fluctuations and provide a clearer picture of underlying trends. By averaging prices over a specific period, moving averages help filter out short-term noise and reveal the broader direction of price movement.Abbreviated as MA, the moving average has long been considered one of the best swing trading indicators in technical analysis. You'll use it to confirm trends in price movement. Because this falls into the category of lagging indicators, you would rarely use the moving average to predict future price movement.

There are two types of moving averages you should be aware of: exponential moving averages (EMA) and simple moving averages (SMA). Both are important, but the exponential moving averages will give you access to the most recent price action.

So, how do you use these moving averages? You'll need to also distinguish between shorter-term MAs and longer-term MAs. Watch for a short-term moving average that crosses a long-term moving average. When this happens, it may be a good time to buy – this is a bullish signal.

While commonly calculated using closing prices, moving averages can also incorporate high and low prices for a more comprehensive view of price action.

Key Types of Moving Averages:

- **Simple Moving Average (SMA):** Calculates the average price over a specified number of periods (e.g., 20 days, 50 days, 200 days).

  - **Pros:** Simple to calculate and understand.

  - **Cons:** Lacks sensitivity to recent price changes due to equal weighting of all data points.

- **Exponential Moving Average (EMA):** Gives more weight to recent prices, making it more responsive to recent price changes.

  - **Pros:** More responsive to market shifts than the SMA.

  - **Cons:** Can be more susceptible to false signals in volatile markets.

- **Weighted Moving Average (WMA):** Assigns greater weight to more recent prices, allowing for a more dynamic response to price changes.

  - **Pros:** More responsive to recent price changes than the SMA, while still providing some smoothing effect.

  - **Cons:** Can be more complex to calculate and interpret.

Utilizing Moving Averages:

Traders often use moving averages to:

- **Identify Trend Direction:** An upward-sloping moving average suggests an uptrend, while a downward-sloping moving average indicates a downtrend.

- **Generate Trading Signals:** Crossovers between different moving averages (e.g., a shorter-term moving average crossing above a longer-term moving average) can generate buy signals, while the opposite crossover can signal a potential sell opportunity.

- **Identify Support and Resistance:** Moving averages can act as dynamic support and resistance levels, providing potential entry and exit points.

Important Considerations:

- **Time Frame Selection:** The choice of the moving average period (e.g., 5-day, 20-day, 50-day) will significantly impact its sensitivity and responsiveness to price changes.

- **Combining with Other Indicators:** Moving averages are often used in conjunction with other technical indicators, such as RSI, MACD, and Bollinger Bands, to enhance trading signals and improve decision-making.

- **Backtesting:** Backtesting trading strategies that utilize moving averages on historical data is crucial to assess their effectiveness and refine your approach.

By understanding the characteristics and applications of different moving averages, traders can gain valuable insights into market trends and make more informed trading decisions.

Moving Averages

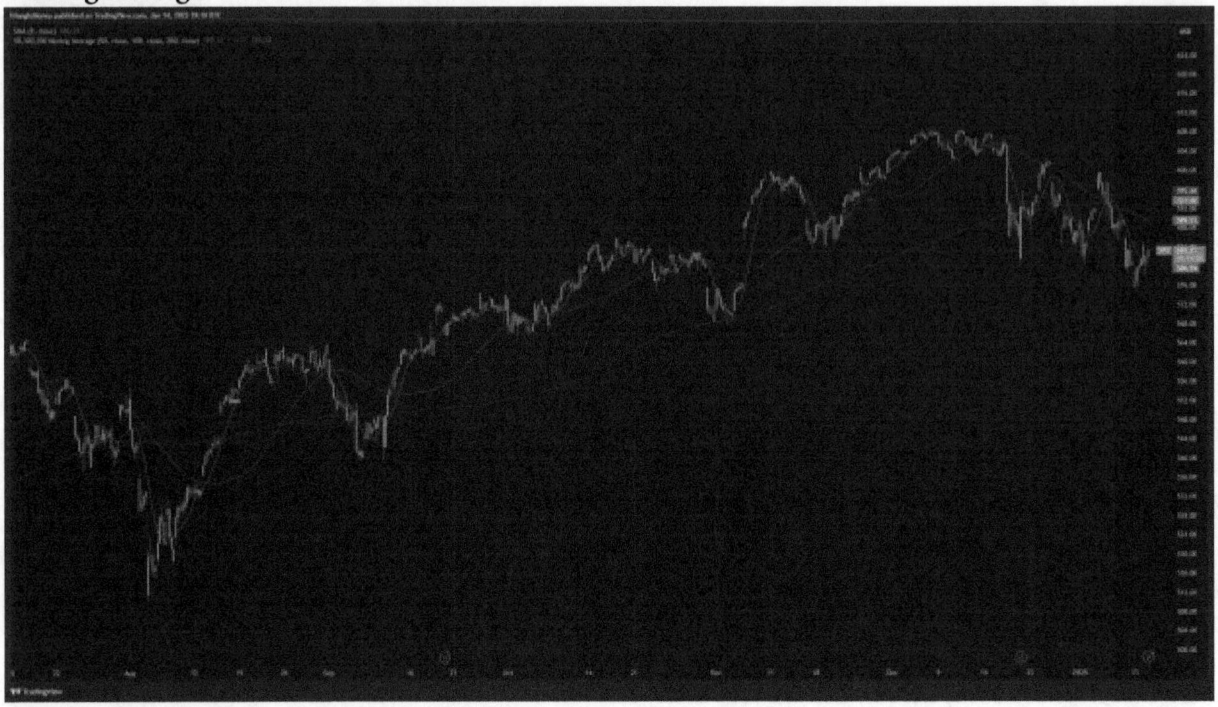

The chart above is the SPY 6 month chart on 2 hour intervals.

Green Line = 50 MA

Blue Line = 100 MA

Red Line = 200 MA

The chart above is brimming with information! It's like a treasure map for navigating the stock market, but only if you know how to read it. I highly recommend taking some time to familiarize yourself with these indicators within your brokerage account.

Think of it like this: your brokerage account is your command center for investing. Just like a pilot needs to know the location of all the controls in the cockpit, you need to understand where to find the information that will help you make informed trading decisions easily.

Ticker symbol SPY which is the index that tracks the S&P 500

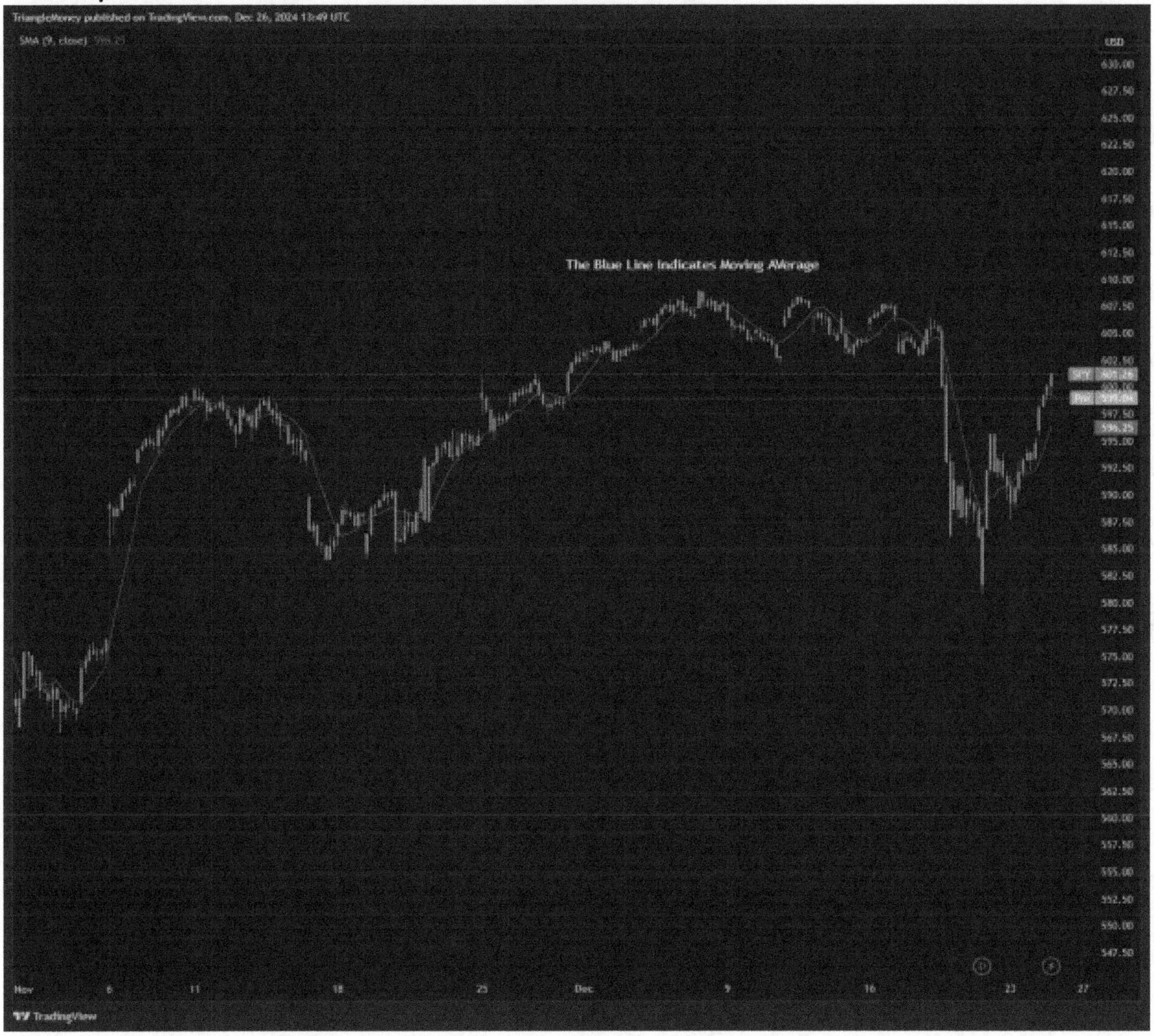

All charts are overflowing with information, a veritable treasure trove for the discerning investor! To truly unlock its potential, you need a trading platform that seamlessly integrates with your analysis.

Choose a platform that allows you to effortlessly overlay indicators on charts. This seemingly simple feature is the cornerstone of effective technical analysis.

Imagine this: you're studying the price action of a stock. By effortlessly overlaying moving averages, you can quickly identify key support and resistance levels. Adding the Relative Strength Index (RSI) helps you gauge the stock's momentum and potential overbought/oversold conditions. And with the MACD (Moving Average Convergence Divergence) indicator, you can pinpoint potential trend changes and divergence signals.

This ability to layer indicators is crucial for:

- **Identifying Trends:** Spotting emerging trends early on can give you a significant edge. By combining moving averages, trendlines, and other indicators, you can accurately identify the direction of price movement.

- **Recognizing Patterns:** Chart patterns, such as head and shoulders, flags, and triangles, often signal potential price reversals or continuations. Overlay the appropriate indicators to confirm these patterns and increase your confidence in trade setups.

- **Making Informed Decisions:** By analyzing the interplay of multiple indicators, you can gain a deeper understanding of market dynamics. This comprehensive analysis empowers you to make more informed trading decisions, whether it's entering a trade, exiting a position, or adjusting your stop-loss orders.

Here's why this is so important:

- **Enhanced Trading Edge:** By combining multiple indicators, you can develop a more robust trading strategy that filters out noise and improves your risk-reward ratio.

- **Increased Confidence:** Analyzing charts with multiple layers of information can increase your confidence in your trading decisions. You're not relying solely on price action, but on a confluence of technical signals.

- **Improved Decision-Making:** By visualizing the interplay of different indicators, you can gain a deeper understanding of market dynamics and make more informed trading decisions.

Remember, the goal is to find a platform that seamlessly integrates with your analysis. Look for platforms with intuitive interfaces, a wide range of customizable indicators, and the ability to easily overlay and adjust them on your charts to best fit your needs.

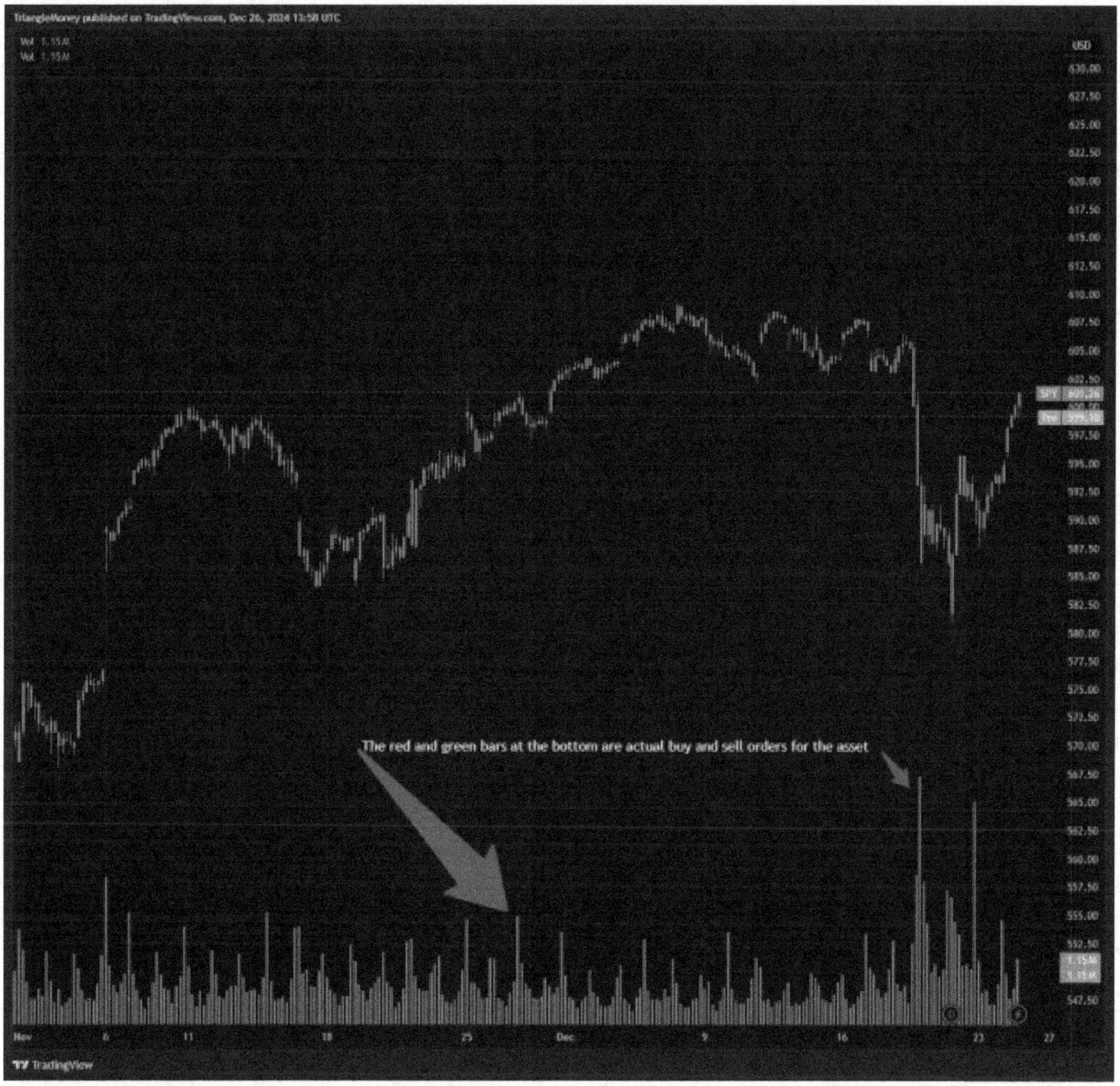

Volume: The Silent Language of the Market

The chart above illustrates the trading volume for the asset you are researching. Depending on your trading strategy, volume can be a significant factor in your decision-making process.

The market has its own unique language and terminology. Understanding these terms is crucial for effective trading. It's not just about whether a stock goes up or down, but rather understanding the 'why' behind price movements.

For example, observe how increased buy volume (often represented by green bars) tends to correlate with rising prices, while increased sell volume (often represented by red bars) typically leads to price declines.

Volume, often overlooked by novice traders, is a crucial indicator that provides valuable insights into the strength and conviction behind price movements. While price tells you *what* is happening, volume reveals *how many* participants are involved and *how strongly* they are acting. Understanding volume is like learning the silent language of the market, allowing you to decipher the true story behind the price action.

What is Volume?

In simple terms, volume represents the total number of shares or contracts traded during a specific period. It's a measure of market activity and participation. High volume indicates strong interest and engagement, while low volume suggests a lack of conviction or indecision among market participants.

What Volume Reveals:
Volume acts as a confirmation or contradiction of price movements. It helps answer crucial questions like:

- **Is this move for real?** A price increase accompanied by high volume suggests strong buying pressure and increases the likelihood that the move is sustainable. Conversely, a price increase on low volume might be a "false breakout" or a temporary blip.

- **Is the trend weakening?** Declining volume during an uptrend can be a warning sign that buying interest is waning, potentially foreshadowing a trend reversal. Similarly, declining volume during a downtrend can suggest that selling pressure is diminishing, which might signal a potential bottom.

- **Where are the key levels?** Areas of high volume often coincide with significant support or resistance levels. These levels represent points where buyers and sellers have clashed in the past, and they can act as important turning points in the future.

- **Is there a shift in sentiment?** A sudden surge in volume can indicate a significant shift in market sentiment, either bullish or bearish. This can be triggered by news events, earnings reports, or other catalysts.

Interpreting Volume:

- **High Volume with Price Increase:** This is generally a bullish signal. It suggests strong buying pressure and increases the likelihood that the price will continue to rise.

- **High Volume with Price Decrease:** This is generally a bearish signal. It indicates strong selling pressure and suggests that the price is likely to continue falling.

- **Low Volume with Price Increase:** This can be a warning sign. It suggests that the price increase is not supported by strong buying interest and may be unsustainable. It could be a "pump and dump" scenario or a temporary move driven by a small number of participants.

- **Low Volume with Price Decrease:** This can also be a warning sign, although less critical. It suggests that the price decrease is not driven by strong selling pressure and may be a temporary correction. However, it's still important to be cautious, as low volume can sometimes precede a larger move.

- **Volume Spikes:** Sudden increases in volume often coincide with significant news events or price breakouts/breakdowns. These spikes can signal a change in trend or a period of increased volatility.

Volume and Trend Analysis:
Volume can be a valuable tool for confirming or contradicting trend signals.

- **Uptrend:** Ideally, volume should increase during rallies and decrease during pullbacks. This indicates that buyers are more enthusiastic than sellers.

- **Downtrend:** Conversely, volume should increase during declines and decrease during bounces. This suggests that sellers are more aggressive than buyers.

Volume and Chart Patterns:

Volume plays a crucial role in validating chart patterns. For example, a breakout from a consolidation pattern is more significant if it's accompanied by a surge in volume. Similarly, a head and shoulders pattern is more reliable if volume is higher during the breakdown than during the formation of the pattern.

Volume Indicators:

Several technical indicators use volume data to provide further insights into market activity. Some popular volume indicators include:

- **On-Balance Volume (OBV):** This indicator attempts to predict price changes based on volume flow.
- **Accumulation/Distribution Line (A/D):** This indicator measures the cumulative volume of buying and selling pressure.
- **Volume Weighted Average Price (VWAP):** This is the average price a security has traded at throughout the day, based on both volume and price.

Imagine a stock breaking out above a key resistance level. If this breakout is accompanied by a significant increase in volume, it's a strong indication that the move is genuine and likely to continue. However, if the breakout occurs on low volume, it's a warning sign that the move may be a "false breakout" and could quickly reverse.

MACD (Moving Average Convergence Divergence)

Another really helpful trend indicator for swing traders is the MACD, or the moving average convergence divergence. This slightly more complex indicator combines the SMA and EMA we discussed above and offers more insights. It helps you confirm a trend while granting you a look into the momentum behind it, too.

MACD calculates the difference between the EMA and SMA. While best practice is to take a 26-period EMA and 12-period SMA, your unique trading style/risk levels may affect the periods you use. You can overlay the MACD on your stock's chart and watch for it to cross above the signal line as a sign that it's time to buy. Conversely, it's time to sell when the MACD crosses under the signal line.

You can also use the MACD to predict reversals. By looking for divergence between the histogram and price action, you can make accurate predictions that a reversal is on the horizon.

RSI (Relative Strength Index)

A pure momentum indicator, the RSI has become the go-to indicator for crypto trading in particular. It helps you identify whether a stock is oversold or overbought based on the magnitude of the price change.

The RSI is displayed as an oscillator. You'll use this line graph to determine where a stock falls on a range from 0-100. A higher number indicates a more overbought stock, while a lower number indicates an oversold stock.

This is a really important indicator to monitor as it can help you get in or out of a stock at the right time. For example – as the RSI climbs above 70, you can assume the stock is overbought and a reversal is on the horizon. Similarly, as the RSI drops below 30, you can predict an upcoming reversal as the bearish trend ends

Technical analysis empowers you with a powerful set of tools to navigate the dynamic world of the financial markets. By mastering the art of chart reading and indicator interpretation, you gain a deeper understanding of market psychology and the forces that drive price movements.

Imagine yourself as a detective, piecing together clues to unravel the market's hidden patterns. Each candlestick, each indicator, provides a valuable piece of the puzzle. By diligently studying charts, identifying key patterns like the ones we've explored, and backtesting your strategies, you'll develop a unique understanding of market behavior.

Remember, this journey is an ongoing process of learning and refinement. There is no single 'holy grail' in trading. Embrace the challenge, experiment with different approaches, and continuously adapt your strategies to the ever-changing market landscape. The rewards for those who dedicate themselves to mastering technical analysis can be substantial, both financially and intellectually.

Chapter 12: Dollar-Cost Averaging: A Disciplined Approach to Trading

Imagine this: you're at the farmer's market, eager to stock up on fresh produce. Do you buy all your groceries from the first vendor you see, regardless of price? Or do you take your time, comparing prices and quality across different stalls? Dollar-Cost Averaging (DCA) is a bit like that – a measured approach to investing that avoids the pitfalls of impulsive market timing.

Instead of plunging into the market with a lump sum, DCA involves systematically investing a fixed amount of money at regular intervals – think of it as a disciplined "drip feed" into your investments. Whether it's weekly, bi-weekly, or monthly, the key is consistency. This unwavering commitment to your investment plan allows you to ride out market fluctuations like a seasoned surfer navigating choppy waves.

The Magic of Averaging Down:

One of the most significant advantages of DCA is its ability to "average down" your purchase price. When the market dips, your fixed investment buys more shares at a lower price. Conversely, when prices soar, you purchase fewer shares, effectively reducing your average cost per share over time. This "buying low, buying less high" strategy can be incredibly powerful in volatile markets, potentially mitigating the impact of sudden price drops.

Conquering the Fear of Market Turmoil:

Let's face it, investing can make you pull your hair out, which explains my bald head. Witnessing market swings can easily trigger fear and uncertainty, tempting you to pull out at the wrong time. DCA, however, can act as a powerful antidote to this fear. By removing the pressure to time the market, you can invest with greater confidence and avoid the emotional pitfalls that often lead to poor investment decisions.

DCA: More Than Just a Strategy, It's a Mindset:

DCA is not just about numbers; it's about cultivating a disciplined investment mindset. It encourages consistent saving and investing, turning it into a regular habit, much like brushing your teeth or going for a run. By automating your investments, you can further simplify the process and ensure you stay on track, regardless of market conditions.

Is DCA Right for You?

While DCA offers numerous benefits, it's not a one-size-fits-all solution.

- **Potential Drawbacks:** If the market consistently rises, you might miss out on some potential gains by not investing the entire sum upfront.

- **Long-Term Perspective:** DCA is best suited for long-term investors with a patient approach.

Dollar-Cost Averaging is a powerful tool that can help you navigate the complexities of the investment world with greater confidence and discipline. By embracing this systematic approach, you can reduce the impact of market volatility, overcome the fear of timing the market, and build a solid foundation for long-term financial success.

Example:

- Imagine you plan to invest $1,000 in a stock over three months.

- If the stock price is $50 in month 1, you buy 20 shares.
- If the price drops to $40 in month 2, you buy 25 shares.
- If the price rises to $60 in month 3, you buy 16 shares.
- Your average cost per share would be lower than if you had invested the whole $1,000 at the beginning.

The Contrarian Approach Trading the Index: A Bird's-Eye View of the Market

Trading the index offers a unique perspective on the market, shifting the focus from individual stocks to the broader performance of a basket of securities. Instead of analyzing the intricacies of a single company, index trading allows you to speculate on the overall direction of a market, sector, or even the global economy. This approach provides diversification and can be a powerful tool for both seasoned traders and those looking for a less company-specific approach to market participation. By understanding the dynamics of index trading, you gain a bird's-eye view of market trends and can position yourself to capitalize on broader economic movements.

The index can guide a contrarian strategy. When the index indicates "Extreme Fear," it suggests excessive pessimism and potentially undervalued assets. This could be a signal to initiate long positions, anticipating a market rebound. Conversely, "Extreme Greed" readings might signal overvaluation, prompting traders to consider short positions or reducing existing long positions.

Identifying Potential Turning Points:

Abrupt shifts in the index can potentially signal significant market shifts. For example, a sudden move from "Extreme Fear" to "Greed" could indicate a potential market reversal. Traders can use this information to time their entries and exits accordingly.

Risk Management: The index can help traders assess overall market risk. High "Fear" readings suggest increased risk aversion, while "Greed" readings may indicate heightened risk appetite. Traders can adjust their position sizes and leverage accordingly based on the prevailing market sentiment.

Important to Know

- **The index is not a perfect predictor.** Market sentiment can remain "Extreme Fear" or "Extreme Greed" for extended periods.
- **False Signals:** The index can generate false signals. It's crucial to combine it with other technical indicators and fundamental analysis for a more robust trading strategy.
- **Diversification:** Even when using the index, diversification across different assets and sectors is essential to mitigate risk.

By carefully incorporating the Fear & Greed Index into your trading strategies, swing traders can potentially improve their risk management, identify potential turning points, and capitalize on market sentiment shifts. However, it's crucial to remember that the index should be used as one tool among many in a comprehensive trading approach.

Chapter 13: Identifying and Trading Price Channels

Channel trading offers a structured approach to navigating price movements within defined boundaries. It's based on the principle that after establishing support and resistance levels, prices often oscillate between them for a period. Mastering channel trading requires understanding how to identify valid channels, the different types, effective trading strategies, and crucial risk management or as I like to call it the tempo.

Identifying Price Channels: A Deeper Dive

- Connecting the Dots: A channel is formed by two parallel (or near-parallel) trendlines. The upper line connects a series of significant highs, acting as resistance. The lower line connects a series of significant lows, acting as support. The more touchpoints the price makes with these lines, the stronger the channel's validity. However, be wary of simply forcing lines to fit; the channel should reflect genuine price action.

- Timeframe Matters: Channels can be observed on any timeframe—from short-term (intraday) charts to long-term (weekly or monthly) charts. Shorter timeframes can offer more frequent trading opportunities but are also prone to more noise and false signals. Longer timeframes generally provide more reliable signals but fewer opportunities.

- Subjectivity and Refinement: Drawing trendlines involves a degree of subjectivity. Different traders might interpret price action slightly differently. Don't be afraid to refine your trendlines as new price data becomes available. A channel isn't static; it evolves.

- Example: Imagine a stock's price repeatedly bouncing off $50 (support) and $55 (resistance). Connecting these points creates a horizontal channel. As the stock continues this behavior, the channel becomes more established.

Types of Price Channels: Beyond the Basics

- Ascending Channel: Characterized by higher highs and higher lows, indicating an uptrend. The support line is typically the stronger of the two lines.

- Descending Channel: Characterized by lower highs and lower lows, indicating a downtrend. The resistance line is typically the stronger of the two lines.

- Horizontal (Sideways) Channel: Indicates a period of consolidation, with no clear upward or downward bias. These channels often precede breakouts or breakdowns.

- Expanding Channel (Less Common): The channel lines diverge, suggesting increasing volatility. These can be trickier to trade.

- Example: A stock consistently making higher highs and higher lows within an upward-sloping channel is exhibiting an ascending channel.

Trading Strategies: Practical Application

- Buy at Support, Sell at Resistance (Within the Channel):

○ *Entry:* Buy when the price touches or comes close to the lower trendline (support). Look for confirming bullish candlestick patterns or indicators.

○ *Stop-Loss:* Place a stop-loss order slightly below the support line to protect against a breakdown.

○ *Target:* Set a price target near the upper trendline (resistance).

• **Breakout Trading (Outside the Channel):**

○ *Entry:* Enter a long position when the price decisively breaks above the upper trendline (resistance) or a short position when it breaks below the lower trendline (support). Look for increased volume to confirm the breakout.

○ *Stop-Loss:* Place a stop-loss order on the opposite side of the broken trendline.

○ *Target:* Project a price target based on the channel's width or other technical analysis methods.

• Trend Following with Channels: Combine channel analysis with the broader trend. For example, if the overall market is bullish, look for ascending channels within individual stocks. Focus on buying at support within these channels.

• Example: If a stock in a horizontal channel breaks decisively above the resistance with strong volume, a breakout trader would buy the stock, anticipating further upside.

Risk and Refinement

• Risk Management: *Always* use stop-loss orders. Channel breakouts can fail, and you need to protect your capital. Position sizing is also crucial. Don't risk more than a small percentage of your trading capital on any single trade.

• Confirmation: Don't rely solely on channels. Use other technical indicators (like RSI, MACD, or volume) to confirm potential trading signals. Divergences between price and indicators can be particularly useful.

• Channel Age: Older, more established channels tend to be more reliable than newly formed ones.

• Volatility: Be aware of market volatility. In highly volatile markets, channels can break down more frequently.

• Example: If a stock is trading in a horizontal channel but the RSI is showing bearish divergence, it might be a warning sign that a breakdown is imminent.

Advantages and Disadvantages: A Balanced View

• Advantages: Clear entry and exit points, defined risk (with stop-loss orders), adaptable to various markets and timeframes.

- Disadvantages: Subjectivity in trendline drawing, potential for false breakouts, not a foolproof strategy.

Conclusion: Practice and Patience

Channel trading can be a valuable tool in a trader's arsenal. However, it requires practice, patience, and a thorough understanding of the concepts involved. Don't rush into live trading before you've backtested your strategies and practiced on a demo account. Remember that no single trading strategy is perfect, and channel trading should be used in conjunction with other forms of technical and fundamental analysis.

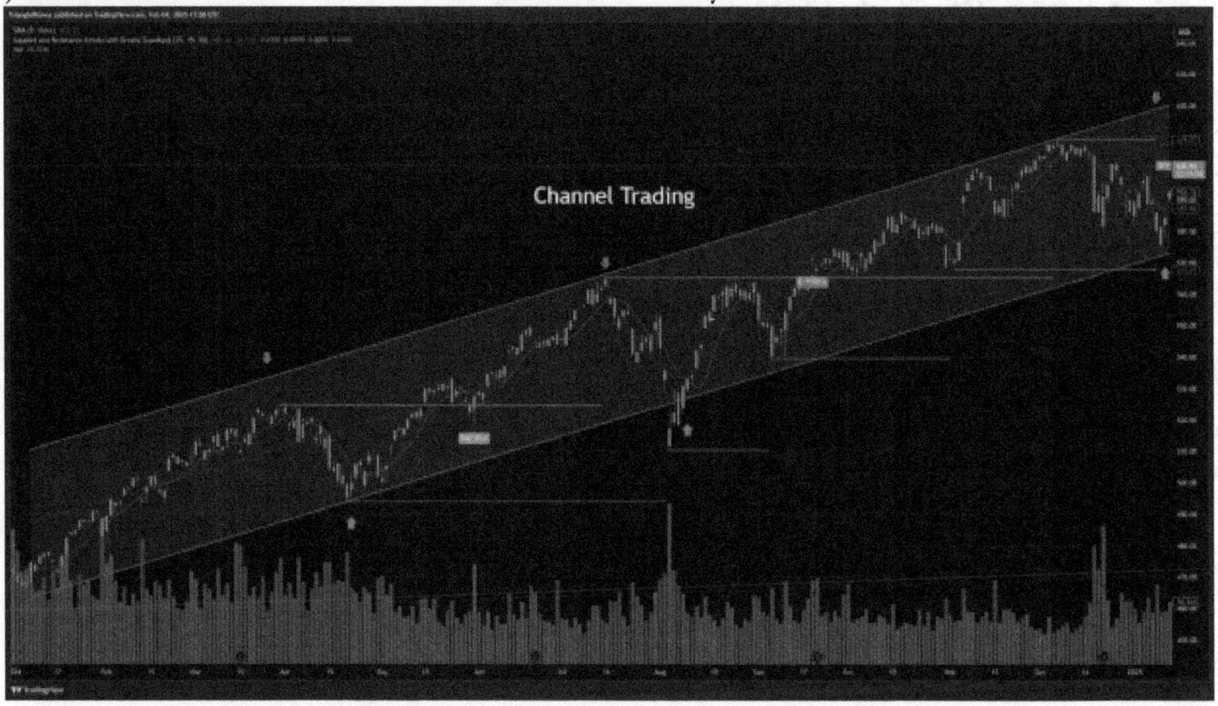

Chapter 14: Decoding the Market's Direction: Mastering Trendlines

Trendlines are a fundamental tool in technical analysis, offering a visual representation of the prevailing direction of price movement. They act as dynamic support and resistance levels, helping traders identify potential entry and exit points, as well as assess the strength and validity of a trend. Mastering the art of drawing trendlines is a crucial skill for any trader seeking to understand and profit from market trends.

What are Trendlines?

A trendline is a straight line drawn on a price chart that connects a series of swing highs (in a downtrend) or swing lows (in an uptrend). These lines help visualize the overall direction of the price movement and act as dynamic support or resistance levels. The underlying principle is that price tends to respect established trendlines, bouncing off them during retracements in an uptrend or encountering resistance at them during rallies in a downtrend.

Drawing Uptrend Lines:

An uptrend line is drawn by connecting a series of successively higher swing lows. At least two lows are required to draw a trendline, but the more points of contact the price makes with the line, the stronger the trendline is considered to be.

1. Identify Swing Lows: Look for two or more distinct low points on the chart where the price has bounced upwards. These are your swing lows.

2. Connect the Lows: Draw a straight line connecting these swing lows. Extend the line into the future to anticipate potential support levels.

3. Refine the Line: As new price data becomes available, you may need to adjust the trendline slightly to ensure it continues to connect significant swing lows. The goal is to have the line touch as many lows as possible without crossing the price action significantly.

Drawing Downtrend Lines:

A downtrend line is drawn by connecting a series of successively lower swing highs. Similar to uptrend lines, at least two highs are needed, but more touchpoints strengthen the trendline.

1. Identify Swing Highs: Look for two or more distinct high points on the chart where the price has reversed downwards. These are your swing highs.

2. Connect the Highs: Draw a straight line connecting these swing highs. Extend the line into the future to anticipate potential resistance levels.

3. Refine the Line: As new price data comes in, adjust the trendline as needed to maintain its connection with significant swing highs.

Key Considerations for Trendline Construction:

- Significance of Swing Points: The swing highs and lows you use to draw trendlines should be significant turning points in the price action, not just minor fluctuations.

- Number of Touchpoints: The more times the price touches the trendline, the stronger and more reliable it is considered to be.

- Angle of the Trendline: Steep trendlines are generally less reliable than shallower ones. Very steep uptrends are often unsustainable and prone to sharp corrections.

- Timeframe Matters: Trendlines can be drawn on any timeframe, from short-term intraday charts to long-term monthly or yearly charts. Longer timeframe trendlines are generally more significant than shorter timeframe ones.

- Subjectivity: Drawing trendlines involves some degree of subjectivity. Different traders might draw slightly different trendlines based on their interpretation of the price action.

Using Trendlines in Trading:

- Identifying Support and Resistance: Uptrend lines act as dynamic support levels, while downtrend lines act as dynamic resistance levels. Traders often look for buying opportunities near uptrend lines and selling opportunities near downtrend lines.

- Confirming Trend Reversals: A break of a trendline can signal a potential trend reversal. A break below an uptrend line suggests a possible shift to a downtrend, while a break above a downtrend line suggests a possible shift to an uptrend.

- Setting Stop-Loss Orders: Trendlines can be used to set stop-loss orders. For example, a trader in a long position might place a stop-loss order just below the uptrend line.

- Identifying Trading Opportunities: Trendlines can help traders identify potential entry and exit points. For example, a trader might enter a long position when the price bounces off an uptrend line and shows signs of strength.

Limitations of Trendlines:

- Subjectivity: As mentioned earlier, drawing trendlines is somewhat subjective. Different traders may draw different trendlines.

- Not Always Reliable: Trendlines are not foolproof. Prices can sometimes break through trendlines, leading to false signals.

- Lagging Indicator: Trendlines are based on past price action, so they are inherently lagging indicators. They confirm a trend after it has already begun.

Combining Trendlines with Other Indicators:

Trendlines are most effective when used in conjunction with other technical analysis tools, such as:

- Moving Averages: Combining trendline analysis with moving averages can provide stronger confirmation of trend reversals.

- Oscillators (RSI, MACD): Using oscillators in conjunction with trendlines can help identify overbought or oversold conditions and potential turning points.

- Chart Patterns: Trendlines can be used to identify and confirm chart patterns, such as triangles, flags, and head and shoulders patterns.

Example:

A stock has been in a confirmed uptrend, repeatedly bouncing off a well-defined uptrend line. The price pulls back to the trendline again, and the RSI shows an oversold condition. This confluence of factors could be a strong signal to enter a long position, anticipating a continuation of the uptrend.

Trendlines are a valuable tool for any trader. They provide a visual representation of market trends and can be used to identify support and resistance levels, confirm trend reversals, and generate trading signals.

While they are not perfect, when used in conjunction with other technical analysis tools and sound risk management practices, trendlines can be a powerful tool for navigating the complexities of the market. Practice is key to mastering the art of drawing and interpreting trendlines. The more you use them, the better you will become at recognizing valid trendlines and using them to your advantage.

Chapter 15: Understanding Fibonacci Retracements: Tools for Predicting Price Reversals

Fibonacci retracements, while powerful, are not a magic bullet. This chapter explores their intricacies, limitations, and how to maximize their effectiveness in your trading strategy.

Refining Fibonacci Application:

• Swing Highs and Lows: The Art of Selection: Accurately identifying swing highs and lows is paramount. Look for significant turning points in the price action, not just minor fluctuations. Consider the context of the overall trend and the timeframe you're analyzing. A swing high/low on a daily chart holds more significance than one on a 5-minute chart.

• Fractal Nature of Markets: Fibonacci retracements can be applied to different degrees of the trend. You can plot retracements on a major uptrend and then also plot retracements on smaller corrections *within* that uptrend. This fractal nature allows you to identify potential entry points at various levels of the market's structure.

• Confluence – The Power of Agreement: The true strength of Fibonacci retracements lies in their confluence with other technical indicators or price action patterns.

○ *Previous Support/Resistance:* If a Fibonacci level coincides with a prior swing high that is now acting as support (in an uptrend) or a prior swing low that is now acting as resistance (in a downtrend), it reinforces the level's importance.

○ *Trendlines:** A Fibonacci retracement level aligning with a trendline break or a trendline acting as support/resistance adds significant weight to the potential reversal.

○ *Chart Patterns:** Look for chart patterns like head and shoulders, double tops/bottoms, or triangles forming near Fibonacci retracement levels. These patterns can provide further confirmation of a potential reversal.

○ *Moving Averages:** Dynamic support/resistance from moving averages (e.g., 20-day, 50-day, 200-day) coinciding with Fibonacci levels can create powerful confluence zones.

○ *Volume:** Increased volume during the retracement and a decrease in volume as the price approaches a Fibonacci level can signal waning momentum of the correction and a potential reversal. Look for a surge in volume upon the bounce or reversal.

Trading Strategies: Advanced Techniques:

• Combining Fibonacci with Candlestick Patterns: Don't just look for the price to touch a Fibonacci level; look for *reversal candlestick patterns* at those levels. Bullish engulfing patterns, hammers, morning stars (for uptrends) and bearish engulfing patterns, shooting stars, evening stars (for downtrends) at Fibonacci levels can provide strong entry signals.

• Fibonacci Extensions: While retracements help identify *potential entry points,* Fibonacci extensions help project *potential price targets.* After establishing a swing high and swing low, use the Fibonacci extension tool to project levels *beyond* the swing high (in an uptrend) or beyond the swing low (in a downtrend). Common extension levels include 127.2%, 161.8%, and 261.8%.

• Fibonacci Clusters: Sometimes, multiple Fibonacci retracement levels from different swings will converge in a small price range, creating a "cluster" of support or resistance. These clusters can be particularly strong reversal zones.

- Using Fibonacci with Elliott Wave Theory: Fibonacci ratios are integral to Elliott Wave theory. They are used to predict the length of various waves within the wave cycle. Combining Fibonacci retracements with Elliott Wave analysis can provide a powerful framework for understanding and trading market movements.

Tempo and Refinement:

- Stop-Loss Placement: Always use stop-loss orders to manage risk. A common strategy is to place the stop-loss slightly below the Fibonacci support level (for long trades) or slightly above the Fibonacci resistance level (for short trades). The exact placement will depend on your risk tolerance and the volatility of the market.

- Confirmation is Crucial: Never blindly enter a trade just because the price has touched a Fibonacci level. Wait for confirmation of a reversal, such as a candlestick pattern, a momentum shift, or a breakout of a short-term counter-trend line.

- Backtesting: Before using Fibonacci retracements in live trading, thoroughly backtest your strategies on historical data. This will help you understand how the tool has performed in the past and identify any potential weaknesses in your approach.

- Adaptability: The market is constantly evolving. Be prepared to adjust your Fibonacci levels and trading strategies as market conditions change.

Here is an Example

A stock is in a confirmed uptrend. It pulls back and touches the 50% Fibonacci retracement level, which also coincides with a rising trendline that has acted as support multiple times. At this level, a bullish hammer candlestick pattern forms. This confluence of Fibonacci retracement, trendline support, and a bullish candlestick pattern provides a strong signal to enter a long position. A stop-loss order is placed below the low of the hammer candlestick.

Fibonacci retracements are a valuable tool for identifying potential turning points in the market. However, they are most effective when used in conjunction with other technical analysis tools and sound risk management practices. Mastering Fibonacci retracements requires practice, patience, and a deep understanding of market dynamics. Don't be afraid to experiment and refine your approach to find what works best for you.

Chapter 16: Decoding Market Signals: Mastering Chart Patterns

Imagine the stock market as a vast ocean, its surface constantly rippling with the ebb and flow of supply and demand. Chart patterns, like intricate sandcastles built by the tide, emerge from this dynamic interplay, offering clues about the market's hidden currents and potential future movements. These visual representations, formed by the interplay of buyers and sellers, are not mere coincidences. They are recurring formations, like fingerprints, that provide valuable insights into market sentiment. By diligently studying these patterns, traders can decipher the market's language, anticipate potential shifts in momentum, and gain a crucial edge in their decision-making. This chapter will delve into the fascinating world of chart patterns, unraveling the mysteries of their formation and exploring their significance in the trading landscape. We will embark on a journey through a diverse array of patterns. We will meticulously examine the characteristics of each pattern, analyze their potential implications for price movement, and discuss strategies for identifying and trading them effectively. By the end of this chapter, you will have a deeper understanding of chart patterns, their significance in market analysis, and how to incorporate them into your own trading arsenal.

Understanding Chart Patterns: A Window into Market Psychology

Chart patterns are visual representations of price action on a stock chart that reveal recurring formations and trends. They reflect the collective psychology of market participants (buyers and sellers) and can provide valuable clues about potential future price movements. However, it's crucial to remember that chart patterns are not guarantees; they are simply probabilities. They should be used in conjunction with other forms of analysis (fundamental analysis, indicator analysis) and sound risk management practices.

Key Considerations When Trading Chart Patterns:

- **Context is Crucial:** A chart pattern's significance depends heavily on the context in which it appears. Consider the overall trend, the volume activity, and other technical indicators before making trading decisions based on a pattern.

- **Confirmation is Key:** Don't jump into a trade solely based on the appearance of a pattern. Wait for confirmation signals, such as a breakout above a trendline or a confirming indicator, before entering a position.

- **Risk Management is Paramount:** "Always check your tempo" Always use stop-loss orders to limit potential losses, regardless of how confident you are in a particular pattern. No pattern is 100% reliable.

- **Practice Makes Perfect:** Learning to identify and trade chart patterns takes time and practice. Use a demo trading account to practice your pattern recognition and trading skills before risking real money.

Major Chart Patterns and Their Interpretation:

Continuation Patterns:

- **Triangles:** Triangles represent periods of consolidation before a breakout. There are three main types:

  - **Symmetrical Triangle:** Neutral pattern, breakout can be bullish or bearish.

  - **Ascending Triangle:** Typically bullish, suggesting an upward breakout.

  - **Descending Triangle:** Typically bearish, suggesting a downward breakout. *(Include clear chart examples for each triangle type)*

- **Flags and Pennants:** Short-term continuation patterns that occur within a strong trend.

  - **Bullish Flag/Pennant:** Indicates a pause in an uptrend before it resumes.

  - **Bearish Flag/Pennant:** Indicates a pause in a downtrend before it resumes. *(Include clear chart examples for each flag/pennant type)*

Reversal Patterns:

- **Head and Shoulders:** A classic bearish reversal pattern that often signals the end of an uptrend. *(Include a clear chart example)*

- **Inverse Head and Shoulders:** A bullish reversal pattern that often signals the end of a downtrend. *(Include a clear chart example)*

- **Double Tops/Bottoms:** These patterns indicate a failed attempt by the price to break through a key resistance or support level, suggesting a potential trend reversal. *(Include clear chart examples for both double top and double bottom)*

- **Rounding Bottom (Saucer):** A long-term bullish reversal pattern that suggests a gradual shift from a downtrend to an uptrend. *(Include a clear chart example)*

- **V-Bottom:** A sharp bullish reversal pattern that indicates a sudden shift from a downtrend to an uptrend. *(Include a clear chart example)*

- **Bullish/Bearish Engulfing:** A two-candlestick pattern that can signal a potential trend reversal. *(Include clear chart examples for both bullish and bearish engulfing)*

- **Morning Star/Evening Star:** Three-candlestick patterns that can signal bullish (morning star) or bearish (evening star) reversals. *(Include clear chart examples for both morning and evening star)*

- **Doji:** A single candlestick pattern that can indicate indecision or a potential trend reversal, especially when it appears at a key support or resistance level. *(Include a clear chart example)*

- **Hanging Man:** A bearish candlestick pattern that appears at the top of an uptrend and can signal a potential reversal. *(Include a clear chart example)*

- **Three Inside Up/Down:** Three-candlestick patterns that can confirm bullish (three inside up) or bearish (three inside down) reversals. *(Include clear chart examples for both three inside up and three inside down)*

- **Three White Soldiers/Three Black Crows:** Three-candlestick patterns that can signal strong bullish (three white soldiers) or bearish (three black crows) reversals. *(Include clear chart examples for both three white soldiers and three black crows)*

Integrating Chart Patterns with Indicators and Trading Platforms:

The ability to overlay indicators onto charts is essential for confirming chart patterns and making informed trading decisions. Explain how indicators like moving averages, RSI, MACD, and volume can be used in conjunction with chart patterns. Discuss the importance of choosing a trading platform that allows for easy integration of indicators and chart patterns.

The Importance of Practice and Patience:

Mastering chart patterns takes time, practice, and patience. Encourage readers to use demo accounts to practice identifying and trading patterns before risking real capital. Emphasize the importance of continuous learning and adapting to changing market conditions.

By restructuring the chapter in this way, you'll provide a much more comprehensive and practical guide to chart patterns, empowering your readers to use them effectively in their trading. Remember to include plenty of real-world chart examples to illustrate each pattern and its interpretation.

Bullish Engulfing

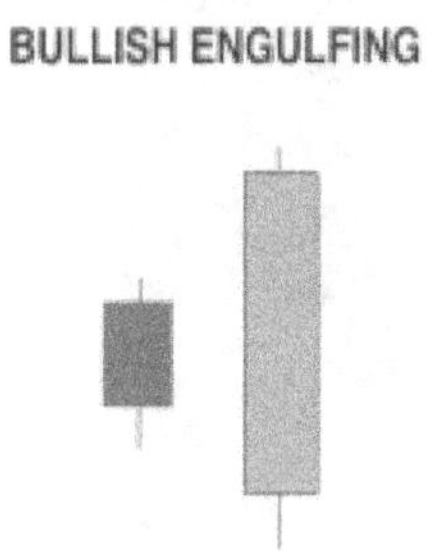

Piercing Line

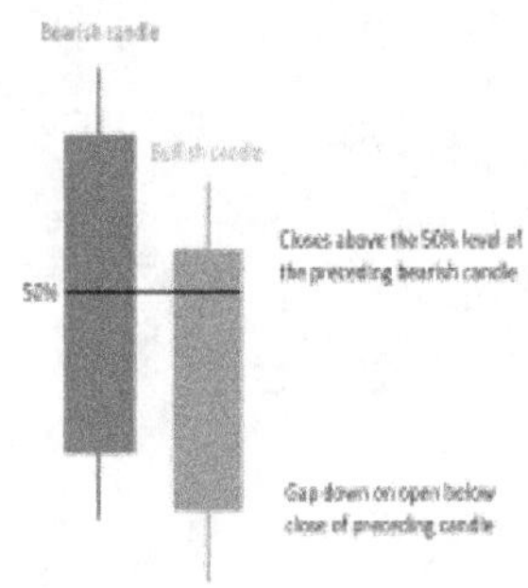

Morning Star

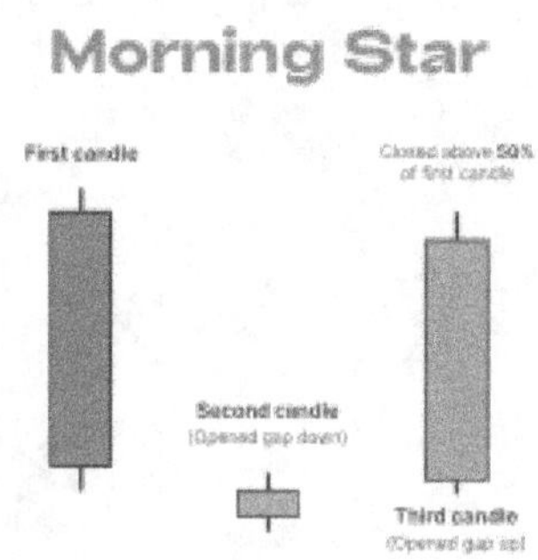

Doji

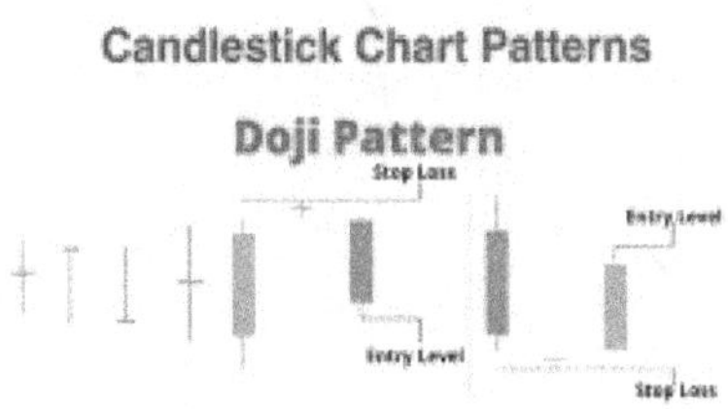

Three White Soldiers

Bullish Harami

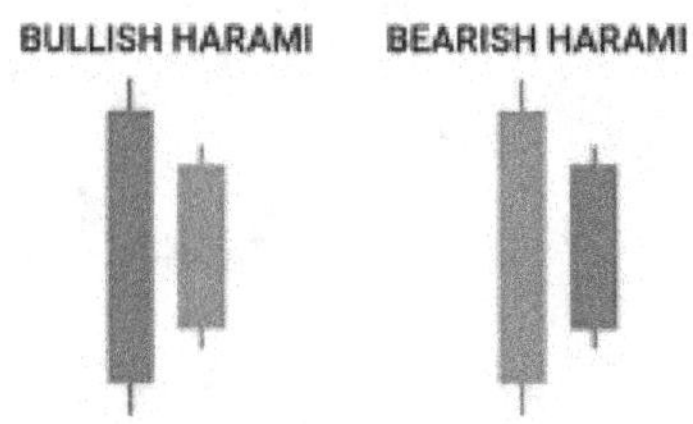

MARKET SYMPHONY
A MUSICIAN'S GUIDE TO TRADING
STOCKS, ETFS, AND DIGITAL ASSETS

Chapter 17: The Battle Lines of the Market: Support and Resistance

Support and resistance levels are fundamental concepts in technical analysis, like the battle lines on a battlefield. They represent price zones where buying or selling pressure tends to concentrate, often causing price reversals. Understanding these levels is absolutely crucial for any trader, as they can provide valuable insights into market dynamics and potential trading opportunities. This chapter will delve deep into the concepts of support and resistance, explaining how to identify them, how to trade them effectively, and what their limitations are.

What are Support and Resistance? The Foundation of Price Action

- **Support:** Imagine a floor that the price of a stock struggles to break through. Support levels are price zones where buying pressure is strong enough to halt or reverse a decline. As a stock's price falls towards a support level, buyers are more likely to enter the market, believing the stock is becoming undervalued. This increased buying pressure can prevent further price declines and potentially push the price back up.

- **Resistance:** Conversely, resistance levels act like a ceiling, preventing prices from rising further. When a stock's price approaches a resistance level, sellers are more likely to enter the market, taking profits or anticipating a price decline. This increased selling pressure can halt or reverse the upward price movement.

Identifying Support and Resistance: Finding the Battle Lines

Support and resistance levels are not always precise lines; they are often zones or areas on a chart. Here are some common methods for identifying these key levels:

- **Previous Price Action:** The most common way to identify support and resistance is by looking at past price action. Areas where the price has repeatedly bounced off or struggled to break through often indicate strong support or resistance. Look for areas where the price has reversed direction multiple times.

- **Trendlines:** Uptrend lines can act as dynamic support levels, while downtrend lines can act as dynamic resistance levels. As long as the price stays above an uptrend line, it's considered to be in an uptrend. A break below the uptrend line could signal a potential trend reversal. The opposite is true for downtrend lines.

- **Moving Averages:** Moving averages can also act as dynamic support and resistance levels. The 20-day, 50-day, and 200-day moving averages are commonly used by traders. When the price is above a moving average, the moving average can act as support. When the price is below a moving average, the moving average can act as resistance.

- **Fibonacci Levels:** Fibonacci retracement levels are based on the Fibonacci sequence and are used to identify potential support and resistance levels.

[1] These levels are often used by traders to predict where a price might retrace after a significant move.

Chapter 18: Long-Term Investing: The Patient Path to Wealth

Long-term investing is the bedrock of wealth creation for countless individuals. It's the "set it and forget it" approach, a strategy perfectly suited for those with a long time horizon (typically three years or more) and a desire for steady, sustainable growth. Imagine planting a seed: you wouldn't expect a towering tree to appear overnight. Instead, you nurture it, providing the necessary resources and patiently waiting for nature to take its course. Long-term investing is much the same, relying on the powerful force of compounding to work its magic over time.

This approach isn't about chasing quick profits or timing the market perfectly. It's about building a portfolio of quality assets and holding them for an extended period, allowing market fluctuations to smooth out and the underlying value of your investments to grow. It's a strategy that favors patience, discipline, and a long-term perspective over short-term gains.

The Power of Compounding: Time is Your Greatest Asset

Compounding is the engine that drives long-term investing. It's the process of earning returns on your initial investment *and* on the accumulated interest or profits from previous periods. Think of it as a snowball rolling downhill, gathering more snow and growing larger with each rotation. The longer your money is invested, the more time it has to compound, and the more significant the final result.

Let's illustrate this with a simple example. Imagine you invest $1,000 in a stock that earns an average annual return of 7%. After one year, you'll have $1,070. In the second year, you'll earn 7% not just on the original $1,000, but also on the $70 you earned in the first year. This may seem like a small difference at first, but over decades, the power of compounding becomes truly remarkable. Small, consistent returns over long periods can lead to substantial wealth accumulation.

Building a Long-Term Portfolio: A Foundation for Success

Constructing a long-term investment portfolio requires careful planning and consideration. Here are some key principles to keep in mind:

- Define Your Goals: What are you investing for? Retirement? A down payment on a house? Your children's education? Clearly defining your goals will help you determine your investment timeframe and risk tolerance.

- Assess Your Risk Tolerance: How much risk are you comfortable taking with your investments? Are you willing to accept potential losses in exchange for the possibility of higher returns? Your risk tolerance will influence the types of assets you choose to include in your portfolio.

- Diversify Your Holdings: Don't put all your eggs in one basket. Diversify your portfolio by investing in a mix of asset classes, such as stocks, bonds, and real estate. Diversification helps reduce risk by spreading your investments across different sectors and industries.

- Invest Regularly: Consistency is key to long-term investing. Make regular contributions to your portfolio, even if it's a small amount. Dollar-cost averaging, a strategy where you invest a fixed amount of money at regular intervals, can help smooth out market volatility and reduce your average cost per share.

- Stay the Course: Market fluctuations are a normal part of investing. Don't panic sell during market downturns. Instead, stay focused on your long-term goals and resist the temptation to make emotional decisions.

- Review and Rebalance: Periodically review your portfolio to ensure it's still aligned with your goals and risk tolerance. You may need to rebalance your portfolio by selling some assets and buying others to maintain your desired asset allocation.

The Benefits of Long-Term Investing:

- Potential for Significant Growth: Over the long term, the stock market has historically delivered strong returns. By investing for the long haul, you can participate in this growth and potentially achieve substantial wealth accumulation.

- Reduced Risk: While short-term market fluctuations can be volatile, the long-term trend of the market has generally been upward. By focusing on the long term, you can reduce the impact of short-term market volatility on your portfolio.

- Simplicity and Convenience: Long-term investing is a relatively simple and hands-off approach. Once you've built your portfolio, you don't need to constantly monitor the market or make frequent trades.

- Tax Advantages: Certain investment accounts, such as 401(k)s and IRAs, offer tax advantages that can further enhance your long-term returns.

A Long-Term Perspective: A Story of Patience

Imagine two investors, Sarah and Tom. Sarah is a long-term investor. She invests regularly in a diversified portfolio of stocks and bonds and holds her investments for decades, weathering market ups and downs. Tom, on the other hand, is a short-term trader. He's constantly buying and selling stocks, trying to time the market perfectly. Over the long term, Sarah's portfolio outperforms Tom's, despite Tom's efforts to beat the market. Sarah's patience and discipline, combined with the power of compounding, ultimately lead to greater wealth accumulation.

Long-term investing is a powerful strategy for building wealth over time. It's a patient, disciplined approach that relies on the magic of compounding and a long-term perspective. By defining your goals, assessing your risk tolerance, diversifying your holdings, and staying the course, you can harness the power of long-term investing to achieve your financial dreams. It's not about getting rich quick; it's about building a solid foundation for long-term financial security.

Long-term investing, as we've discussed, is about cultivating wealth over an extended period, allowing the power of compounding to work its magic. Your approach, separating long-term investments into a dedicated account and focusing on emerging and growing industries, adds a layer of strategic foresight. It's like planting a diverse orchard, with some established trees (ETFs and dividend stocks) providing consistent yields, while others (emerging industry picks) represent the potential for explosive growth in the future.

The Hunt for the Next Big Thing: Riding the Wave of Innovation

In my Long-Term investing Ifocus on emerging and growing industries is a hallmark of forward-thinking long-term investing. It's about identifying disruptive technologies, groundbreaking innovations, or shifts in consumer behavior *before* they become mainstream. It's about anticipating future trends and positioning your portfolio to capitalize on that growth. This approach carries higher risk, as emerging industries are inherently more volatile and uncertain. However, the potential reward – finding the "next big company" – can be substantial.

Think of the early investors in companies like Apple, Amazon, or Tesla. They recognized the potential of these companies before most of the market did, and their long-term investments paid off handsomely. Your strategy is similar, seeking to identify those future market leaders in their nascent stages.

Due Diligence and Research: The Cornerstone of Emerging Industry Investing

Investing in emerging industries requires extensive due diligence and research. It's not enough to simply follow the hype. You need to delve deep into the industry, understand the competitive landscape, assess the company's management team, and evaluate its technology or product. Here are some key areas to focus on:

- Industry Analysis: What are the key trends driving growth in this industry? What are the potential challenges and risks?

- Competitive Landscape: Who are the other players in this space? What are their strengths and weaknesses? How does the company you're considering differentiate itself?

- Financials: While financial performance may not be the primary focus for early-stage companies, it's still important to assess their burn rate, cash flow, and funding runway.

- Management Team: Who is leading the company? Do they have the experience and expertise to execute their vision?

- Technology/Product: Is the company's technology or product truly innovative? Does it have the potential to disrupt the market?

ETFs and Dividend Reinvestment: Building a Solid Foundation

Your strategy of including ETFs and dividend stocks in your long-term portfolio provides a solid foundation. ETFs offer instant diversification across a specific sector, industry, or even the entire market. They're a low-cost and efficient way to gain exposure to a broad range of assets.

Dividend stocks, on the other hand, provide a stream of income that can be reinvested to purchase more shares, a process known as *dividend reinvestment* or DRIP. This allows you to capitalize on the power of compounding even further. By reinvesting your dividends, you're essentially using your earnings to buy more "seeds," which will then generate more earnings, creating a snowball effect over time.

The Power of Compounding: Amplified by DRIP

Let's illustrate the power of dividend reinvestment with an example. Imagine you own 100 shares of a stock that pays a 3% annual dividend. If you take the cash dividends, you'll receive $300 per year. However, if you reinvest those dividends, you'll use the $300 to buy more shares of the stock. Over time, as you accumulate more shares through dividend reinvestment, your dividend income will grow, and your portfolio will compound even faster.

Chapter 19: Preserving Your Capital: The Art of Position Sizing

This chapter delves into the critical concept of position sizing, a cornerstone of risk management that can make or break your trading career. It's not just about avoiding ruin; it's about optimizing your returns while protecting your capital.

What is Position Sizing? The Key to Risk Control

Position sizing is the process of determining the appropriate number of shares or contracts to buy or sell in a single trade. It's about finding the sweet spot between maximizing potential profits and limiting potential losses. Effective position sizing allows you to control the amount of risk you take on each trade, ensuring that no single losing trade can significantly damage your trading capital.

Why is Position Sizing So Important? More Than Just Survival

- **Capital Preservation:** The primary purpose of position sizing is to protect your trading capital. By limiting the amount you risk on any single trade, you can avoid the dreaded "blown account" scenario.

- **Consistent Returns:** Proper position sizing allows you to achieve more consistent returns over time. It prevents large losses from wiping out your profits and helps you maintain a smoother equity curve.

- **Emotional Control:** When you know your risk is controlled, you're less likely to make emotional trading decisions. You can trade with more confidence and discipline, knowing that even a losing trade won't be catastrophic.

- **Optimal Risk-Reward Ratio:** Position sizing plays a crucial role in achieving your desired risk-reward ratio. By adjusting your position size, you can ensure that your potential profit on a trade outweighs your potential loss.

Factors Affecting Position Size: A Multifaceted Calculation

Several factors influence your ideal position size. It's not a one-size-fits-all calculation.

- **Account Size:** Your total trading capital is a fundamental factor. Larger accounts can generally handle larger positions (but not necessarily proportionally larger risk).

- **Risk Tolerance:** This is your personal comfort level with potential losses. Are you conservative, moderate, or aggressive? A conservative trader will risk a smaller percentage of their capital per trade than an aggressive trader. *This is a psychological factor and needs to be carefully considered.*

- **Stop-Loss Level:** Your stop-loss order (the price at which you will automatically exit a trade to limit losses) is a critical component of position sizing. The closer your stop-loss is to your entry price, the larger your position size can be (for a given risk level).

- **Market Volatility:** More volatile securities require smaller position sizes to maintain the same risk level. High volatility means the price can move quickly and unexpectedly, increasing the potential for larger losses.

- **Investment Style/Time Horizon:** Long-term investors typically have larger position sizes (relative to their account) than day traders because they're less concerned with short-term price fluctuations.

Calculating Position Size: The Math Behind Risk Management

Here are a couple of common methods for calculating position size:

- **Percentage Risk Method:** This is the most popular method and the one I recommend. You decide what percentage of your trading capital you are willing to risk on any single trade (e.g., 1%, 2%). Then, you calculate your position size based on your stop-loss level and the stock's price.

○ **Formula:** Position Size = (Account Size * Risk Percentage) / (Entry Price - Stop-Loss Price)

○ **Example:** You have a $10,000 account and are willing to risk 1% per trade. You are buying a stock at $50 with a stop-loss at $45.

Position Size = ($10,000 * 0.01) / ($50 - $45) = $100 / $5 = 20 shares

- **Fixed Dollar Amount Method:** You decide on a fixed dollar amount you're willing to risk per trade, regardless of your account size. This method is less flexible than the percentage risk method but can be simpler to implement.

○ **Formula:** Position Size = Fixed Dollar Amount / (Entry Price - Stop-Loss Price)

○ **Example:** You are willing to risk $200 per trade. You are buying a stock at $50 with a stop-loss at $45.

Position Size = $200 / ($50 - $45) = $200 / $5 = 40 shares

My aggressive 10-13% Rule: A Good Starting Point, But...

My rule of never risking more than 10-13% of my capital on a single trade is a *very aggressive* approach. While it might work for some experienced traders, it's generally not recommended for beginners. A more conservative approach, such as risking 1-2% per trade, is usually more appropriate, especially when you're still learning and developing your trading skills. As you gain experience and confidence, you can gradually adjust your risk percentage. **The Perils of a 10-13% Risk Per Trade:**

Risking such a substantial portion of your capital on a single trade introduces several significant problems:

- **Elevated Risk of Ruin:** The probability of losing a significant portion, or even all, of your trading capital increases dramatically with such high risk per trade. A few losing trades in a row can decimate your account, leaving you with insufficient funds to continue trading. This is the dreaded "risk of ruin."

- **Amplified Emotional Stress:** The potential for large losses creates intense emotional pressure. Fear and greed become amplified, leading to impulsive decisions, chasing losses, and an inability to stick to your trading plan. This emotional rollercoaster hinders clear thinking and effective trading.

- **Hindered Learning and Development:** When you're constantly worried about large losses, your focus shifts from learning and improving to simply trying to avoid disaster. This can impede your progress as a trader and prevent you from developing sound trading habits.

- **Reduced Statistical Probability of Success:** Even if you have a winning strategy, the high risk per trade significantly reduces the probability of you surviving long enough to see the statistical edge play out. A string of inevitable losing trades can wipe you out before your strategy has a chance to become profitable over the long run.

The Prudent Path: The 1-2% Rule and Beyond:

The 1-2% rule is a cornerstone of responsible risk management. It dictates that you should never risk more than 1-2% of your *total trading capital* on a single trade. This seemingly small percentage makes a world of difference:

- **Capital Preservation:** Small, controlled losses are far less damaging than large, infrequent ones. The 1-2% rule allows you to weather losing streaks and preserve your capital for future opportunities.

- **Emotional Control:** Lower risk reduces emotional stress, promoting more rational decision-making. You're less likely to panic or make impulsive choices when the potential loss is manageable.

- **Focus on Learning:** With less emotional pressure, you can concentrate on analyzing your trades, identifying areas for improvement, and refining your trading strategy.

- **Statistical Advantage:** By limiting your risk, you increase your chances of surviving long enough to see the statistical edge of your trading strategy play out.

Adapting the 1-2% Rule to Your Trading Style:

I hold a concentrated portfolio of less than 10 stocks and maintain a substantial cash reserve. This approach can be effective, but it requires careful risk management. Here's how you can integrate the 1-2% rule:

1. **Calculate Your Risk Tolerance:** Determine the maximum percentage of your *total* trading capital you're willing to lose on a single trade. Start conservatively with 1% and gradually increase it *only* as you gain experience and consistently demonstrate profitability.

2. **Position Sizing is Key:** Once you've determined your risk tolerance, calculate the appropriate position size for each trade. Here's the formula:

   ○ Risk Amount (in dollars) = Total Trading Capital * Risk Percentage

   ○ Number of Shares = Risk Amount / Price per Share

3. **Stop-Loss Orders: Your Safety Net:** Always use stop-loss orders to automatically exit a trade when it moves against you. The stop-loss order should be placed at a price that corresponds to your predetermined risk amount. For example, if you're risking $100 on a trade and you're buying a stock at $50, your stop-loss should be placed at a price where a sale of your shares will result in a $100 loss.

4. **Portfolio Diversification (Even with a Concentrated Approach):** While you hold less than 10 stocks, ensure they're diversified across different sectors or industries. This helps mitigate the risk of a single event significantly impacting your entire portfolio.

Gradually Increasing Risk:

As you gain experience, consistently demonstrate profitability, and thoroughly understand risk management, you *might* consider gradually increasing your risk per trade. However, this should be done with extreme caution. Even experienced traders rarely risk more than a small percentage (e.g., 2-5%) of their capital on a single trade. Never jump from 1-2% to 10-13% – this is a recipe for disaster.

The 10-13% risk per trade is far too aggressive for most traders, especially beginners. Adhering to the 1-2% rule is essential for capital preservation, emotional control, and long-term success in trading. Combine this with proper position sizing, stop-loss orders, and diversification (even within a concentrated portfolio), and you'll be well on your way to a more sustainable and profitable trading career. Remember, trading is a marathon, not a sprint. Focus on long-term growth and capital preservation, not short-term gains at the expense of excessive risk.

No Blown Accounts: A Goal, Not a Guarantee

While proper position sizing significantly reduces the risk of blowing up your account, it doesn't eliminate it entirely. Market conditions can change rapidly, and unexpected events can happen. The goal is to manage risk effectively, not to eliminate it completely. Even with the best position sizing strategy, you will still experience losing trades. The key is to ensure that those losing trades don't jeopardize your entire trading capital.

Position sizing is not just a mathematical calculation; it's a mindset. It's about taking a responsible and disciplined approach to trading, understanding that risk management is just as important as profit potential. By mastering the art of position sizing, you can significantly improve your chances of long-term success in the markets.

Chapter 20: The $600 Lesson

My trading journey began, as it does for many, with a fervent, almost manic, enthusiasm. I devoured every piece of information I could find about technical indicators, eager to unlock the secrets of the market. The problem wasn't a lack of information, but rather an overabundance. My charts resembled a Jackson Pollock painting – a chaotic explosion of RSI, every moving average imaginable, volume indicators, Fibonacci retracements, MACD, and my own hand-drawn trend lines, all vying for attention. It was a visual cacophony, a confusing mess of lines and colors that somehow, inexplicably, had led me to a ten-trade winning streak.

Looking back, I realize just how precarious my situation was. My financial foundation was practically non-existent. My emergency savings account held a meager $100, and my brokerage account, the source of my newfound "success," contained only $600. This was my first, and perhaps most significant, mistake. I was playing with fire, risking virtually everything on the volatile whims of the market. Rent was due in eight days, and despite having a job, I was still $400 short. Instead of simply transferring the money from my brokerage account to cover the shortfall, a sensible and responsible action, I decided to try and grow my trading capital. Flush with the confidence of my winning streak, I convinced myself I could make up the difference in the market.

This decision, fueled by a dangerous mix of arrogance and desperation, set the stage for disaster. I spotted a "promising" trade and, true to form, proceeded to plaster my chart with every indicator I could find. The sheer volume of information overwhelmed me, blurring my judgment and even obscuring my understanding of a clear exit price. I took on more risk than I should have, a violation of the rudimentary rules I was beginning to formulate (but not consistently following). My trading plan, at this point, was more of a suggestion than a disciplined strategy.

I placed my order, setting a three-day timeframe for the trade to play out. This single trade was supposed to solve all my problems – covering the rent shortfall and padding my portfolio. Day one saw the stock trade sideways, confined to a tight range. I glued myself to the screen, a hawk watching for any sign of a breakout, but nothing happened. Day two brought a glimmer of hope: the stock opened 2% higher. Surely, this was it! But again, the price languished, going nowhere. Another day, another disappointment.

Day three, the final day of my self-imposed timeframe, dawned with a jolt. The stock price jumped at the market open, sending my hopes soaring. I held on, anticipating the breakout, when suddenly, a large red candle materialized on the screen. The stock was plummeting, and fast. Panic seized me. I had neglected to set a stop-loss, a critical error that would soon prove devastating. My internet connection seemed to slow to a crawl as I frantically tried to exit the trade. By the time my sell order went through, I had lost a staggering 30% of my capital. Just like that, my $600 stake had shrunk significantly. The very moment I needed it most, the market turned against me.

The consequences were immediate and painful. I was forced to liquidate my entire brokerage account to cover the remaining rent shortfall. The $600 lesson had been brutally delivered.

The aftermath of this trade was a period of intense reflection. I learned several crucial lessons, lessons etched in the pain of financial loss. First and foremost, I understood the absolute necessity of a solid financial foundation before venturing into the world of trading. Trading while living paycheck to paycheck is a recipe for disaster. It creates a vicious cycle where trading profits are constantly siphoned off to pay bills, hindering any chance of building capital.

The importance of a stop-loss order was another hard-won lesson. Had I set a stop-loss, even a tight one, I could have salvaged at least a small profit from day two's 2% rise, potentially avoiding the need to liquidate my account entirely.

Finally, I revisited the chart of that ill-fated trade, now stripped of its overwhelming clutter of indicators. As I methodically deleted each one, something remarkable emerged. The 2% rise on day two, the one I had completely missed, coincided precisely with a major Fibonacci retracement level. This crucial signal had been completely obscured by the sheer volume of other indicators, a victim of my own overcomplication. The $600 lesson taught me the value of simplicity, the power of a solid financial foundation, and the critical importance of risk management. It was a painful but invaluable experience that shaped my approach to trading from that day forward.

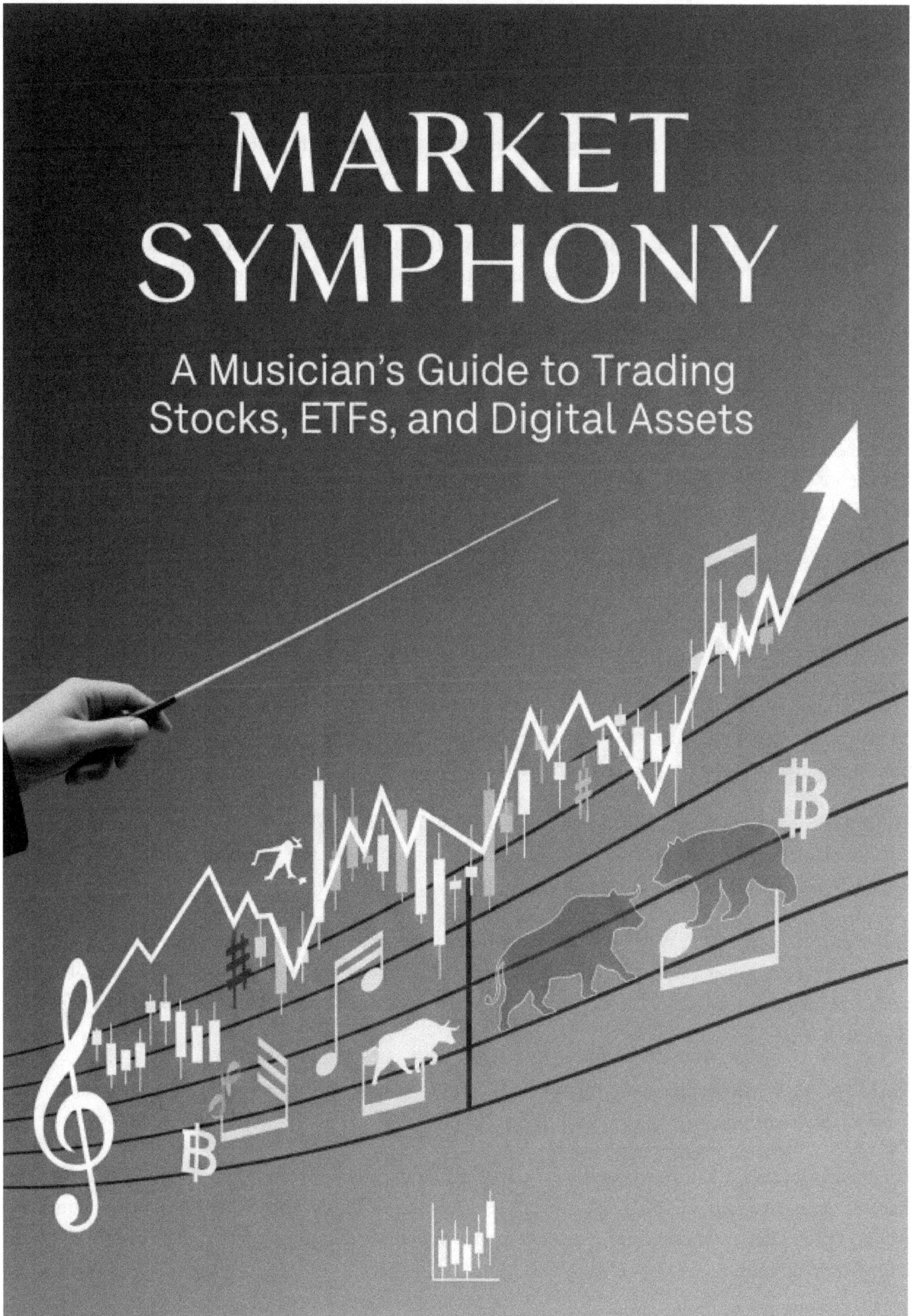
MARKET
SYMPHONY
A Musician's Guide to Trading
Stocks, ETFs, and Digital Assets

Chapter 21: Your Trading Blueprint: Crafting a Winning Trade Plan and Journal

This chapter provides a comprehensive guide to developing a robust trade plan and maintaining a detailed trading journal – two essential tools for any serious trader. These aren't just good ideas; they're the cornerstones of consistent profitability and long-term success.

Part 1: Your Trade Plan: Charting Your Course to Success

A well-defined trade plan is your roadmap to navigating the complexities of the market. It's a personalized set of rules and guidelines that dictate your trading decisions, helping you stay disciplined and avoid emotional pitfalls. Think of it as your business plan for trading.

Why is a Trade Plan So Crucial? Discipline in the Face of Volatility

- Eliminates Emotional Trading: A trade plan helps you avoid impulsive decisions driven by fear, greed, or hope.
- Manages Risk: It defines clear entry and exit points, stop-loss orders, and position sizing rules, protecting your capital.
- Promotes Consistency: A well-defined plan fosters a consistent approach, increasing the probability of long-term success.
- Builds Confidence: Having a plan provides a sense of control and composure, especially during market volatility.
- Facilitates Learning and Growth: By tracking your trades and analyzing your performance against your plan, you can identify areas for improvement and refine your strategy.

Key Components of a Successful Trade Plan: Your Personalized Guide

Your trade plan should be tailored to your individual circumstances, risk tolerance, and trading style. Here's a breakdown of the essential elements:

- Trading Philosophy (Your "Why"): What is your overall approach to trading? Are you a long-term investor, swing trader, or day trader? What are your investment goals (financial independence, supplemental income, etc.)? What is your risk tolerance (conservative, moderate, aggressive)? *This is the foundation upon which your entire plan is built.*
- Trading Style: Which trading style will you employ (long-term investing, swing trading, day trading)? *This decision flows directly from your trading philosophy.*
- Goals and Objectives: Define specific, measurable, achievable, relevant, and time-bound (SMART) goals. What are your financial targets (e.g., annual return, capital appreciation)? What is your target win percentage? *Be realistic and avoid setting unrealistic expectations.* Break down your goals into monthly, yearly, and long-term targets.
- Markets Traded: Which markets will you focus on (stocks, forex, crypto, commodities)? *Consider your knowledge and experience when choosing markets.*

• Timeframes: Which timeframes will you use for analysis and trading decisions (e.g., daily, weekly, hourly)? *This is crucial for aligning your trading style with your available time and risk tolerance.*

• Setups (Your "Playbook"): What specific chart patterns, technical indicators, or fundamental criteria will you use to identify trading opportunities? *This is where you define your "edge" in the market.* Document specific entry triggers and the rationale behind them.

• Entry Rules: Clearly define the precise conditions that must be met before you enter a trade. *Be specific and avoid vague criteria.*

• Stop-Loss Rules: Determine where you will place your stop-loss order to limit potential losses. *This is non-negotiable. Protecting your capital is paramount.* Base your stop-loss on technical levels, volatility, or a percentage of your capital at risk.

• Exit/Take Profit Rules: Define your profit targets and exit strategies. Will you use fixed profit targets, trailing stops, or a combination of both? *Have a clear plan for taking profits. Don't let greed keep you in a trade longer than you should be.*

• Risk Management Rules: Specify the maximum percentage of your trading capital you are willing to risk on a single trade and overall. *This is the most important part of your plan. Never risk more than you can afford to lose.*

• Pre-Market Routine: Describe your pre-market activities, such as research, watchlist creation, and market analysis. *Preparation is key to successful trading.*

• Post-Market Routine: Outline your post-market activities, including reviewing your trades, analyzing your performance, and updating your trading journal. *This is where you learn and improve.*

• Tools and Resources: List the tools and resources you will use for your trading business (brokerage platform, charting software, news feeds, etc.).

• Review Process: Establish a schedule for reviewing and updating your trade plan. *Your plan should be a living document that evolves with your experience and market conditions.*

• Continuing Education: Outline your plan for continuing education, such as reading books, attending webinars, or taking courses. *The market is constantly evolving, so continuous learning is essential.*

• Discipline and Mindset Notes: Include notes on your psychological approach to trading, addressing potential emotional biases and strategies for maintaining discipline. *Trading psychology is just as important as technical skills.*

• Golden Rules/Trading Commandments: List your most important trading rules and principles. *These are the non-negotiable rules you will always follow.* This could include rules about withdrawals, dividend reinvestment (DRIP), asset reevaluation, or any other personal financial considerations.

Part 2: Your Trading Journal: A Window into Your Performance

A trading journal is an invaluable tool for self-reflection and continuous improvement. It's a detailed record of your trading activity, capturing not only the technical details of each trade but also your thought processes, emotions, and the market context.

Why is a Trading Journal So Important? Learning from Your Experiences

- Performance Tracking: Identify winning strategies and spot recurring mistakes.
- Improved Discipline: Journaling enforces accountability and promotes consistent trading habits.
- Emotional Control: Recognize and address emotional biases that impact your decision-making.
- Continuous Learning: Adapt to market changes and refine your trading approach.

Key Elements of a Comprehensive Trading Journal: Documenting Your Journey

- Trade Details:
  - Date and Time (Entry and Exit)
  - Instrument (Stock Symbol, etc.)
  - Trade Type (Long or Short)
  - Entry Price
  - Exit Price
  - Position Size
  - Stop-Loss Order Price
  - Take-Profit Target (if used)
- Trade Rationale:
  - Reason for Entry (Technical, Fundamental, News, etc.)
  - Market Conditions (Bullish, Bearish, Sideways)
- Trade Management:
  - Plan Adherence (Did you follow your plan?)
  - Emotional State (Fear, Greed, Excitement, etc.)
- Post-Trade Analysis:
  - Profit/Loss
  - Risk-Reward Ratio
  - Self-Reflection (What went well? What could be improved?)
  - Lessons Learned
- Additional Notes:
  - Relevant News or Events
  - Market Commentary
  - Personal Notes

Tips for Effective Journaling: Making the Most of Your Records

- Be Consistent: Update your journal after every trade, no matter how small.
- Be Honest: Acknowledge your mistakes and biases.
- Be Detailed: Provide as much relevant information as possible.
- Be Objective: Analyze your trades without emotional bias.
- Review Regularly: Periodically review your journal to identify patterns and areas for improvement.
- Use Technology: Spreadsheets, trading journal apps, or even a simple notebook can be effective tools. Find what works best for you.

Combining Your Trade Plan and Journal: A Powerful Synergy

Your trade plan and journal work together in a powerful synergy. Your trade plan provides the structure and guidelines for your trading, while your journal allows you to track your execution of that plan and learn from your experiences. By consistently using both tools, you can significantly increase your chances of trading success.

Your "Playbook": Developing Your Signature Strategies

As you gain experience and analyze your journal, you will begin to identify trading strategies that consistently work for you. These are your "go-to" trades, your bread and butter. Document these strategies in your trade plan, creating your own personal "playbook" of winning trades.

By following the advice in this chapter, you'll be well on your way to developing a robust trade plan and maintaining a valuable trading journal. These tools are not just helpful; they are essential for any trader who wants to achieve consistent profitability and long-term success. Remember, trading is a business, and like any successful business, it requires planning, discipline, and a commitment to continuous improvement.

MARKET
SYMPHONY
A Musician's Guide to Trading
Stocks, ETFs, and Digital Assets

Chapter 22: Testing Your Trading Strategies: The Power of Backtesting

Before risking real capital in the live market, backtesting your trading ideas and strategies is absolutely essential. It's like a flight simulator for pilots, allowing you to test your skills and refine your approach without the risk of crashing. This chapter will guide you through the backtesting process, highlighting its benefits, limitations, and best practices.

Why Backtest? Validating Your Trading Ideas

Backtesting involves applying your trading strategy to historical market data to simulate how it would have performed in the past. This process allows you to:

- **Identify Potential Flaws:** Uncover weaknesses or inconsistencies in your trading rules.
- **Optimize Parameters:** Refine your entry and exit criteria, stop-loss levels, and position sizing.
- **Evaluate Performance:** Assess key metrics like win rate, average win/loss ratio, maximum drawdown, and overall return.
- **Gain Confidence:** Build confidence in your strategy by seeing how it has performed under various market conditions.

The Backtesting Process: A Step-by-Step Guide

1. **Data Collection:** Gather high-quality historical data for the assets you plan to trade. The more data you have, the more robust your backtest will be. Ensure the data is clean, accurate, and covers a sufficient time period (ideally several years). Consider data frequency (daily, hourly, etc.) and ensure it aligns with your trading style.

2. **Strategy Formulation:** Clearly define all the rules and parameters of your trading strategy. Be specific and avoid vague terms.

    - **Entry Rules:** Specify precise triggers for entering a trade (e.g., "Buy when the price closes above the 50-day moving average with RSI above 50").
    - **Exit Rules:** Define clear profit targets and stop-loss levels.
    - **Position Sizing:** Determine how much capital you will risk per trade (e.g., 1% of your account).
    - **Risk Management Rules:** Outline your overall risk tolerance and how you will manage risk.

3. **Platform Selection:** Choose a backtesting platform or software. Many trading platforms offer basic backtesting capabilities. Dedicated backtesting software or programming languages like Python offer more advanced features and customization.

4. **Strategy Implementation:** Translate your trading rules into a format that the backtesting platform can understand. This may involve using the platform's scripting language or coding your own backtesting program.

5. **Simulation and Analysis:** Run the backtest simulation on the historical data. The platform will simulate how your strategy would have performed, generating performance metrics.

6. **Performance Evaluation:** Carefully analyze the results. Don't just focus on the overall return. Consider these key metrics:

○ **Win Rate:** Percentage of winning trades.

○ **Average Win/Loss Ratio:** The ratio of average profit to average loss.

○ **Maximum Drawdown:** The largest peak-to-trough decline in your account equity during the backtest.

○ **Profit Factor:** Gross profit divided by gross loss.

○ **Sharpe Ratio:** Risk-adjusted return.

7. **Strategy Refinement:** Based on the results, refine your strategy. This might involve adjusting your entry/exit rules, position sizing, or risk management. Repeat the backtesting process until you are satisfied with the results.

Beyond the Numbers: Understanding the "Why"

Don't just chase high returns. Analyze *why* your strategy performed the way it did. Look at individual trades, both winners and losers. Identify patterns and trends. Consider how your strategy would have handled different market conditions.

The Limitations of Backtesting: Past Performance is Not a Guarantee

Backtesting is a valuable tool, but it's not a crystal ball. Remember these crucial limitations:

- **Past Performance:** Past performance is not indicative of future results. Market conditions change, and a strategy that worked well in the past may not work in the future.

- **Data Limitations:** Historical data may not perfectly reflect the complexities of the live market. Factors like slippage, commissions, and unexpected events can impact real-world performance.

- **Curve Fitting:** Be careful not to over-optimize your strategy to fit the historical data perfectly. This can lead to poor performance in live trading.

- **Psychological Factors:** Backtesting cannot replicate the emotional pressures of live trading. Fear and greed can significantly impact your decisions in the real world.

Paper Trading: A Useful Tool, But Not a Substitute

Paper trading (simulated trading) can be helpful for familiarizing yourself with a trading platform and testing the *mechanics* of a strategy. However, it has significant limitations:

- **Lack of Emotional Realism:** Paper trading cannot replicate the fear and greed that come with risking real money. This can lead to overconfidence and unrealistic expectations.

- **Distorted Risk Perception:** Traders may take more risks in paper trading because there are no real consequences.

My Perspective on Paper Trading:

My personal experience with paper trading is not good. It's important to acknowledge that the lack of emotional involvement can create a disconnect from the realities of live trading. While paper trading has its place, it shouldn't be relied upon as a primary method for testing trading strategies. Paper trading takes the emotion of the wins and losses away from the trader.

The Importance of Continuous Learning and Adaptation:

The market is constantly evolving. No trading strategy will work perfectly all the time. Be prepared to continuously learn, adapt, and refine your approach based on your backtesting results, paper trading experience, and live market performance.

Testing Your Way to Trading Success

Backtesting is a critical step in developing a successful trading strategy. It allows you to test your ideas, identify potential flaws, and optimize your approach before risking real money. However, it's important to be aware of the limitations of backtesting and not rely on it as a guarantee of future success. Combine backtesting with paper trading and a commitment to continuous learning to maximize your chances of achieving your trading goals.

Chapter 23: The $380 Lesson: How Bad Position Sizing Can Wreck Your Trading

My early foray into day trading served as a brutal but valuable lesson in the critical importance of position sizing. It's a lesson I paid for dearly – $380 to be exact. Remember I have 7 children in my home so losing any amount of money is a huge blow to the household. My story is a cautionary tale, highlighting how even a seemingly "lucky" win can set you up for a devastating fall if you don't understand risk management. What is the tempo?

My $380 Mistake: A Cautionary Tale

Like many beginners, I was drawn to the allure of quick profits in day trading. I had $350 in my account and, based on a hunch (not research), I bought two $1.00 out-of-the-money options contracts. I didn't fully grasp that each contract controlled 100 shares, however I entered the trade anyway. My $200 investment represented a huge chunk of my capital.

By sheer luck, the stock price moved in my favor off of its earnings announcement, and I quickly sold the contracts for a $170 profit. I felt like a genius! I had nearly doubled my money in seconds. This early win, however, was the worst thing that could have happened to me. It gave me a false sense of confidence and skewed my perception of risk.

The next day, I repeated the same mistake. I bought two *more expensive* out-of-the-money call options, investing $400 of my $520 account balance. This time, my "hunch" was wrong. The stock price plummeted after earnings, and my $400 investment shrunk to a measly $20. I had lost 77% of my trading capital in a single trade.

The Realization: Position Sizing is King

This devastating loss was a wake-up call. It drove home the critical importance of position sizing. I realized that I wasn't a "trading genius"; I was just lucky the first time. My problem wasn't my stock picking; it was my reckless risk management.

What is Position Sizing, and Why Does It Matter?

Position sizing is the process of determining the appropriate number of shares or contracts to buy or sell in a single trade. It's the most important tool you have for controlling risk and preserving your capital. It's not just about avoiding ruin; it's about optimizing your returns while managing risk effectively.

- **Capital Preservation:** Position sizing protects your trading capital from devastating losses.
- **Consistent Returns:** It helps you achieve more consistent returns by limiting the impact of losing trades.
- **Emotional Control:** Knowing your risk is controlled reduces emotional trading.
- **Optimal Risk-Reward Ratio:** Position sizing helps you achieve your desired risk-reward ratio.

How to Calculate Position Size: The Math of Risk Management

Here are the two most common methods for calculating position size:

- **Percentage Risk Method (Recommended):** Determine the percentage of your trading capital you're willing to risk on a single trade (e.g., 1%, 2%). Then, calculate your position size based on your stop-loss level and the stock's price.

  - **Formula:** Position Size = (Account Size * Risk Percentage) / (Entry Price - Stop-Loss Price)
  - **Example:** You have a $1,000 account and risk 1% per trade. You buy a stock at $50 with a stop-loss at $45.

Position Size = ($1,000 * 0.01) / ($50 - $45) = $10 / $5 = 2 shares

- **Fixed Dollar Amount Method:** Decide on a fixed dollar amount you're willing to risk per trade.
  - **Formula:** Position Size = Fixed Dollar Amount / (Entry Price - Stop-Loss Price)
  - **Example:** You risk $50 per trade. You buy a stock at $50 with a stop-loss at $45.

Position Size = $50 / ($50 - $45) = $50 / $5 = 10 shares

The Importance of a Stop-Loss Order:

A stop-loss order is a crucial part of position sizing. It's an order to automatically sell your position when the price reaches a certain level, limiting your potential losses. Your stop-loss level should be based on technical analysis, volatility, or a percentage of your capital at risk.

Risk Tolerance: Finding Your Comfort Zone

Your risk tolerance is your personal comfort level with potential losses. Are you conservative, moderate, or aggressive? A conservative trader will risk a smaller percentage of their capital per trade (e.g., 1%) than an aggressive trader (e.g., 2%). *It's crucial to be honest with yourself about your risk tolerance.*

Treating Trading Like a Business:

Your approach to treating trading like a business is excellent. Professional traders have a plan, a system, and a focus on risk management.

- **Trading Plan:** A written trading plan is essential. It should outline your trading strategies, risk management rules, entry and exit criteria, and performance goals.
- **Discipline:** Stick to your trading plan and avoid emotional decisions.
- **Continuous Learning:** The market is constantly changing. Commit to continuous learning and improvement.

Quick Riches: A Dangerous Trap

The promise of quick riches is a major draw to trading, but it's also a dangerous trap. As you pointed out, social media is full of stories of overnight millionaires, but these stories rarely tell the whole truth. Successful trading is not about luck; it's about skill, discipline, and risk management.

Realism and Expectations:

It's important to have realistic expectations. Even successful traders rarely achieve daily returns of more than a few percentage points. Focus on consistent, long-term growth, not get-rich-quick schemes.

Control Your Risk, Control Your Destiny

My $380 loss taught me a valuable lesson about the power of position sizing. It's a lesson I've never forgotten. By mastering this crucial aspect of risk management, you can significantly improve your chances of success in the challenging world of trading. Remember, it's not about how much you can win; it's about how much you can *not lose*.

MARKET SYMPHONY
A MUSICIAN'S GUIDE TO TRADING
STOCKS, ETFS, AND DIGITAL ASSETS

Chapter 24: The Probability of a Down Month, Quarter, or Year – and How to Stay Motivated

The market, like the weather, is prone to fluctuations. Just as we experience sunny days and stormy nights, the financial markets ebb and flow, presenting periods of growth alongside inevitable downturns. Understanding the probability of experiencing a down month, quarter, or even year is crucial for managing expectations, mitigating risk, and, perhaps most importantly, maintaining the motivation necessary to navigate the challenging times.

The Inevitability of Downturns:

Let's be clear: down periods are not anomalies; they are a normal and expected part of the market cycle. Trying to predict the precise timing of these downturns is a fool's errand. Even the most seasoned investors and analysts can't consistently forecast market movements. Instead of attempting to time the market, a more pragmatic approach involves understanding the historical context and accepting the inherent uncertainty.

While past performance is not indicative of future results, historical data can offer some insights. Analyzing long-term market trends reveals that corrections, bear markets, and periods of volatility are recurring events. The frequency and severity of these downturns vary, but their presence is a constant. Studying these historical patterns can provide a valuable perspective, reminding us that market fluctuations are a natural part of the investment landscape.

Understanding Probabilities (and Their Limitations):

While we can analyze historical data to understand the frequency of down periods, it's essential to recognize the limitations of probability in the context of the market. The market is a complex adaptive system influenced by countless factors, including economic conditions, geopolitical events, investor sentiment, and even unforeseen black swan events. These factors interact in unpredictable ways, making it impossible to assign precise probabilities to future market movements.

For instance, while historical data might suggest that a market correction occurs, on average, every few years, this doesn't guarantee that a correction is due or that it will necessarily occur within a specific timeframe. The market can remain irrational for longer than you can remain solvent, as the saying goes. Therefore, it's crucial to avoid relying solely on historical probabilities to make investment decisions.

Staying Motivated Through the Storm:

Perhaps the most significant challenge during market downturns is maintaining motivation. Seeing your portfolio shrink can be disheartening, especially if you're a new investor or if you're relying on your investments for income. However, it's during these challenging times that a long-term perspective and a disciplined approach are most critical.

Here are some strategies for staying motivated during market downturns:

- Focus on your long-term goals: Remember why you started investing in the first place. Whether it's retirement, a down payment on a house, or financial independence, keeping your long-term goals in sight can help you weather short-term volatility.

- Don't panic sell: One of the biggest mistakes investors make during market downturns is panic selling. Selling low locks in losses and prevents you from participating in the eventual market recovery. Instead, try to resist the urge to react emotionally and stick to your investment plan.

- Rebalance your portfolio: Market downturns can be an opportune time to rebalance your portfolio. If certain assets have declined more than others, you can sell some of the relatively better-performing assets and buy more of the underperforming ones, effectively buying low and setting yourself up for potential gains when the market recovers.

- View downturns as opportunities: Instead of viewing market downturns as a threat, try to see them as opportunities. Lower prices mean that you can buy assets at a discount. Warren Buffett famously said, "Be fearful when others are greedy, and greedy when others are fearful."

- Stay informed, but don't obsess: It's important to stay informed about market developments, but constantly checking your portfolio and consuming news can amplify anxiety. Set aside specific times to review your investments and avoid constantly monitoring the market.

- Seek professional advice: If you're feeling overwhelmed or uncertain, consider consulting with a financial advisor. A qualified advisor can help you develop a sound investment strategy and provide guidance during market downturns.

- Remember that markets recover: Historically, markets have always recovered from downturns. While the duration and severity of each downturn vary, the overall trend has been upward over the long term. Keeping this historical perspective in mind can help you stay motivated and avoid making rash decisions.

Two Stories of Resilience:

To illustrate the importance of maintaining a long-term perspective and avoiding panic selling, consider these two hypothetical stories:

Story 1: The Disciplined Investor:

Sarah began investing for retirement in her early 30s. She diligently contributed to her 401k and maintained a diversified portfolio of stocks and bonds. When the market experienced a significant downturn in 2008, Sarah was understandably concerned. However, she remembered her long-term goal of retiring comfortably and resisted the urge to sell. Instead, she viewed the downturn as an opportunity to buy more shares at lower prices. She continued to contribute regularly and rebalanced her portfolio as needed. When the market eventually recovered, Sarah's portfolio rebounded strongly, putting her back on track for her retirement goals.

Story 2: The Emotional Investor:

John started investing around the same time as Sarah. He was initially excited about the potential for market gains, but he was also easily swayed by market news and sentiment. When the 2008 downturn hit, John panicked. He sold all of his stocks, locking in significant losses. He then moved his money to what he perceived as safer investments, like cash and bonds. While these investments provided some stability, they didn't participate in the subsequent market recovery. John missed out on substantial gains and fell behind on his retirement savings.

These stories highlight the critical role of emotional control and a long-term perspective in navigating market downturns. The disciplined investor, like Sarah, understands that market fluctuations are inevitable and uses them to their advantage. The emotional investor, like John, allows fear and panic to drive their decisions, often leading to costly mistakes.

Conclusion:

Experiencing down months, quarters, and even years is an unavoidable part of investing. Understanding the probability of these downturns, while recognizing the limitations of predicting their exact timing, is crucial for managing expectations and mitigating risk. By focusing on long-term goals, avoiding panic selling, and viewing downturns as potential opportunities, investors can stay motivated and navigate the inevitable storms of the market cycle, ultimately increasing their chances of achieving their financial objectives. Remember, successful investing is a marathon, not a sprint.

Chapter 25: The Ironclad Rule: Mastering the Tempo for Trading Success

Before you even think about profits, risk management must be your top priority. It's not just about minimizing losses; it's about ensuring your survival and long-term success in the challenging world of trading. This chapter will provide you with the essential tools and techniques to master risk management and protect your trading capital.

Why Risk Management is Paramount: More Than Just Avoiding Ruin

Risk management is the foundation of successful trading. It's not just about avoiding big losses; it's about:

- Capital Preservation: Protecting your trading capital from devastating losses.
- Consistent Profitability: Enabling consistent returns by minimizing the impact of losing trades.
- Emotional Control: Reducing the emotional stress of trading and preventing impulsive decisions.
- Long-Term Sustainability: Ensuring your trading career is sustainable over the long haul.

Know Your Enemy: Understanding the Downside

Before entering any trade, ask yourself: "What's the worst that could happen?" This isn't pessimism; it's realistic risk assessment. Determine the maximum amount you're willing to lose on *this specific trade*. This requires a clear understanding of your stop-loss level and position size.

Your Shield: The Stop-Loss Order (Revisited)

A stop-loss order is your most important risk management tool. It's a predetermined exit point that automatically closes your position if the price moves against you. Think of it as an insurance policy for your trades.

- Types of Stop-Loss Orders:
    - Market Stop: Executes at the next available price. Can result in slippage (getting a worse price than expected) in volatile markets.
    - Limit Stop: Executes only at your specified price or better. May not fill if the price moves quickly past your limit.
    - Trailing Stop: Adjusts the stop-loss level as the price moves in your favor, locking in profits and limiting potential losses.
- Where to Place Your Stop-Loss:
    - Technical Levels: Place your stop-loss below a key support level or above a key resistance level.

○ Volatility: Use volatility measures (like Average True Range - ATR) to determine an appropriate stop-loss distance.

○ Percentage of Capital: Risk a fixed percentage of your trading capital per trade (e.g., 1%, 2%).

The Risk-Reward Ratio: A Guiding Principle

The risk-reward ratio compares the potential profit of a trade to the potential loss. A favorable risk-reward ratio (e.g., 2:1, 3:1) means that your potential profit is greater than your potential loss. Strive for trades with a favorable risk-reward profile to improve your odds of long-term profitability.

- Calculating the Risk-Reward Ratio:

○ Risk-Reward Ratio = (Profit Target - Entry Price) / (Entry Price - Stop-Loss Price)

○ Example: You buy a stock at $50 with a profit target of $60 and a stop-loss at $48.

Risk-Reward Ratio = ($60 - $50) / ($50 - $48) = $10 / $2 = 5:1

Position Sizing: The Foundation of Risk Control (Expanded)

Position sizing is crucial for managing risk. It determines how many shares or contracts you should trade based on your risk tolerance and stop-loss level. *This is where you put your risk management principles into action.*

- Percentage Risk Method (Recommended): Risk a fixed percentage of your trading capital per trade (e.g., 1%, 2%).

○ Formula: Position Size = (Account Size * Risk Percentage) / (Entry Price - Stop-Loss Price)

○ Example: $1,000 account, 1% risk per trade, buy at $50, stop-loss at $45.

Position Size = ($1,000 * 0.01) / ($50 - $45) = $10 / $5 = 2 shares

- Fixed Dollar Amount Method: Risk a fixed dollar amount per trade.

○ Formula: Position Size = Fixed Dollar Amount / (Entry Price - Stop-Loss Price)

Diversification: Don't Put All Your Eggs in One Basket

Diversify your portfolio across different asset classes, sectors, and individual securities to reduce your overall risk. Don't concentrate your capital in a single trade or a small number of stocks.

Managing Risk During a Trade: Staying Flexible

- Monitoring: Continuously monitor your trades and be prepared to adjust your stop-loss level or exit a trade if market conditions change.

- Emotional Control: Avoid emotional decisions. Stick to your trading plan and don't let fear or greed influence your actions.

Common Risk Management Mistakes to Avoid:

- Not Using Stop-Loss Orders: This is a recipe for disaster. Always use stop-loss orders to protect your capital.

- Ignoring Position Sizing: Trading too large a position can lead to significant losses, even if your win rate is high.

- Chasing Losses: Don't try to "get even" after a losing trade. Stick to your trading plan and don't increase your risk.

- Overtrading: Excessive trading can lead to increased commissions and emotional fatigue, negatively impacting your performance.

- Ignoring Market Conditions: Be aware of market volatility and adjust your risk accordingly.

Risk Management is Your Edge

Risk management is not just a set of rules; it's a mindset. It's about prioritizing the preservation of your capital and ensuring your long-term survival in the markets. By mastering risk management, you're not just minimizing losses; you're maximizing your chances of achieving consistent profitability and trading success. It's the most important skill you can develop as a trader.

Chapter 26: Navigating the Market: Stocks, Options, and the Power of Diversification

This chapter explores the distinct characteristics of stocks and options, two fundamental instruments in the trading world. It also emphasizes the critical role of diversification in building a resilient and profitable portfolio.

Part 1: Stocks vs. Options: Understanding the Differences

Stocks and options offer fundamentally different ways to participate in the market. Understanding their unique characteristics, risks, and rewards is essential for making informed investment decisions.

Stocks: Ownership and Participation

When you buy a stock, you become a part-owner of the company. You have a claim on its assets and earnings, and you can participate in its growth (or decline).

- **Key Characteristics:**
  - Ownership of a portion of the company.
  - Potential for long-term capital appreciation.
  - Dividend payments (for some stocks).
  - Voting rights on company matters.
- **Advantages:**
  - Relatively simple to understand.
  - Potential for long-term growth.
  - Can generate income through dividends.
- **Disadvantages:**
  - Can be volatile in the short term.
  - Risk of losing your entire investment if the company fails.

Options: Rights and Obligations

Options are contracts that give you the *right,* but not the *obligation,* to buy or sell an underlying asset (usually a stock) at a specific price (the strike price) on or before a specific date (the expiration date).

- **Key Characteristics:**
  - Contractual agreements, not ownership.
  - Leverage: Small price movements in the underlying asset can lead to large percentage gains (or losses) in the option price.
  - Time decay: Options lose value over time, especially as the expiration date approaches.
- **Types of Options:**
  - **Call Options:** Give you the right to *buy* the underlying asset.
  - **Put Options:** Give you the right to *sell* the underlying asset.

- **Advantages:**
  - Leverage: Amplifies potential gains.
  - Flexibility: Can be used for various strategies (hedging, speculation, income generation).
- **Disadvantages:**
  - High risk: Potential for significant losses, including the entire premium paid for the option.
  - Time decay: Options lose value over time.
  - Complexity: Options strategies can be complex and require a deep understanding of their mechanics.

Which is Right for You?
The choice between stocks and options depends on your individual investment goals, risk tolerance, and knowledge.

- **Stocks:** Generally suitable for long-term investors seeking capital appreciation and/or dividend income.
- **Options:** More appropriate for experienced traders who understand the complexities and risks involved.

My Approach:
My personal approach of allocating a smaller portion of your portfolio to options (15%) while focusing primarily on stocks is a common and sensible strategy. It allows you to explore the potential benefits of options while limiting your overall risk.

Part 2: The Power of Diversification: Reducing Risk and Enhancing Returns
Diversification is a cornerstone of sound investment practices. It's about spreading your investments across different assets, sectors, and asset classes to reduce risk and enhance returns. It's like not putting all your eggs in one basket.
Why Diversify? Mitigating Risk and Maximizing Potential

- **Reduces Portfolio Volatility:** Diversification helps to smooth out the ups and downs of your portfolio. When one investment performs poorly, others may be performing well, offsetting the losses.
- **Minimizes Unsystematic Risk:** Unsystematic risk is the risk associated with a specific company or industry. Diversification reduces your exposure to this type of risk.
- **Improves Risk-Adjusted Returns:** Diversification can help you achieve a higher return for a given level of risk.
- **Protects Against Unexpected Events:** Diversification can help protect your portfolio from unforeseen events, such as economic downturns or geopolitical crises.

Key Diversification Strategies:

- **Asset Allocation:** Spreading your investments across different asset classes (stocks, bonds, real estate, commodities).

- **Sector Diversification:** Investing in companies from various sectors of the economy (technology, healthcare, consumer staples, etc.).

- **Geographic Diversification:** Investing in companies from different countries and regions.

- **Security Selection:** Diversifying within each asset class by investing in a range of companies or securities.

Sectors Matter: Understanding the Economic Landscape

The 11 major sectors provide a useful framework for understanding the stock market and building a diversified portfolio. (Expand on each sector with more detail about its characteristics, typical companies, and how it performs in different economic cycles.)

1. **Consumer Discretionary:** This sector consists of companies that produce goods and services that are not considered essential, such as apparel, automobiles, and restaurants. Examples include companies like Nike, Ford, and McDonald's.
2. **Consumer Staples:** This sector includes companies that produce essential goods and services, such as food, beverages, and household products. Companies like Procter & Gamble, Coca-Cola, and Walmart fall into this sector.
3. **Energy:** This sector comprises companies involved in the exploration, production, and distribution of energy, such as oil and gas companies. ExxonMobil, Chevron, and ConocoPhillips are examples of companies in this sector.
4. **Financials:** This sector includes companies that provide financial services, such as banks, insurance companies, and investment firms. Think of companies like JPMorgan Chase, Bank of America, and Berkshire Hathaway.
5. **Health Care:** This sector consists of companies that provide healthcare services and products, such as pharmaceuticals, medical devices, and healthcare providers. Johnson & Johnson, Pfizer, and UnitedHealth Group are examples of companies in this sector.
6. **Industrials:** This sector includes companies that produce capital goods, such as machinery, transportation equipment, and aerospace and defense products. Companies like Boeing, Caterpillar, and General Electric belong to this sector.
7. **Information Technology:** This sector comprises companies that develop and provide technology-related products and services, such as software, hardware, and semiconductors. Companies like Apple, Microsoft, and Intel are in this sector.
8. **Materials:** This sector includes companies that produce raw materials, such as chemicals, metals, and construction materials. Companies like Dow Chemical, Freeport-McMoRan, and Nucor are examples of companies in this sector.
9. **Real Estate:** This sector consists of companies that own, develop, and manage real estate, such as real estate investment trusts (REITs). Companies like Simon Property Group and Prologis are in this sector.
10. **Utilities:** This sector includes companies that provide essential utilities, such as electricity, gas, and water. Companies like Duke Energy, Southern Company, and American Water Works are examples of companies in this sector.

Understanding these sectors is important for investors because it allows them to diversify their portfolios and make informed investment decisions based on the performance of different sectors.

Size Matters: Large-Cap, Mid-Cap, and Small-Cap Stocks

Market capitalization (market cap) is the total dollar value of a company's outstanding shares. It's a key factor to consider when diversifying your portfolio.

- **Large-Cap Stocks:** (Market cap over $10 billion) Generally considered more stable and less volatile.
- **Mid-Cap Stocks:** (Market cap between $2 billion and $10 billion) Offer a balance between growth potential and stability.
- **Small-Cap Stocks:** (Market cap under $2 billion) Higher growth potential but also higher risk and volatility.

Key Considerations for Diversification:

- **Diversification does not guarantee profits or eliminate the risk of loss.** It's about managing risk, not eliminating it.
- **Over-diversification can dilute returns and increase costs.** Don't spread your investments too thin.
- **The effectiveness of diversification depends on the correlation between the different assets in your portfolio.** Choose assets that are not perfectly correlated.

Building Your Diversified Portfolio: A Personalized Approach

The ideal diversification strategy depends on your individual investment goals, risk tolerance, and time horizon. Consider your personal circumstances and consult with a financial advisor if needed.

A Balanced Approach to Market Participation

Understanding the differences between stocks and options, along with the power of diversification, is crucial for building a successful investment portfolio. By taking a balanced approach and tailoring your strategy to your individual needs, you can increase your chances of achieving your financial goals.

Chapter 27: Finding Your Diamonds in the Rough: Mastering Stock Screeners

Now that you've funded your trading account and developed a trading plan, it's time to find the stocks that fit your criteria. Stock screeners are powerful tools that can help you sift through the vast universe of publicly traded companies and identify potential trading opportunities quickly and efficiently. This chapter will guide you through the process of using stock screeners effectively, helping you find the "diamonds in the rough."

Fundamental vs. Technical Analysis: Your Approach to Stock Selection

Before diving into screeners, it's essential to understand the two primary approaches to stock analysis:

- **Fundamental Analysis:** Examining a company's financial health, competitive landscape, and market position. This involves analyzing financial statements (balance sheet, income statement, cash flow statement), key ratios (P/E, price-to-book, ROE), and qualitative factors (management quality, competitive advantages). Fundamental analysis is crucial for long-term investing.

- **Technical Analysis:** Predicting future price movements based on historical price charts and market data. Technical analysts use various indicators (moving averages, RSI, MACD) and chart patterns to identify trends and potential trading opportunities. Technical analysis is more commonly used by short-term traders.

My Approach:

I use 85% technical / 15% fundamental approach is common among active traders. Many traders use technical analysis to identify entry and exit points, while using fundamental analysis to filter for fundamentally sound companies.

Stock Screeners: Your Filtering Powerhouse

Stock screeners are online platforms that allow you to filter stocks based on specific criteria. They significantly reduce the time and effort required to find potential investments that match your strategy.

Key Features of Stock Screeners:

- **Customizable Filters:** Define specific criteria based on your investment goals and risk tolerance.

- **Data-Driven Insights:** Access a wealth of financial data, including price, volume, financial statements, and analyst ratings.

- **Time-Saving:** Quickly filter through thousands of stocks to create a manageable list of candidates.

- **Backtesting Capabilities (Some Screeners):** Test your screening criteria against historical data.

How to Use Stock Screeners Effectively: A Step-by-Step Guide

1. **Define Your Criteria:** Before using a screener, you must know what you're looking for. This comes from your trading plan. Are you looking for growth stocks, value stocks, dividend stocks, or something else? What are your preferred technical indicators or fundamental metrics?

2. **Choose a Screener:** Several stock screeners are available, both free and paid. Some popular options include those offered by brokerage platforms (e.g., TD Ameritrade's thinkorswim, Fidelity's Active Trader Pro), Finviz, TradingView, and others. Experiment with different screeners to find one that suits your needs.

3. **Input Your Criteria:** Enter your desired criteria into the screener. Be specific and use a combination of filters to narrow down your search. Here are some common screening criteria:

○ **Fundamental Criteria:**

- Market Capitalization (Large-cap, Mid-cap, Small-cap)
- Price-to-Earnings Ratio (P/E)
- Price-to-Sales Ratio (P/S)
- Price-to-Book Ratio (P/B)
- Earnings Growth
- Revenue Growth
- Profit Margin
- Return on Equity (ROE)
- Debt-to-Equity Ratio
- Dividend Yield
- Free Cash Flow

○ **Technical Criteria:**

- Price (Above/Below certain moving averages)
- Volume (Average daily volume)
- Relative Strength Index (RSI)
- Moving Average Convergence Divergence (MACD)
- Stochastic Oscillator

- Chart Patterns (e.g., breakouts, consolidations)
- Volatility (Average True Range - ATR)

4. **Refine Your Search:** Start with a broader set of criteria and gradually narrow it down until you have a manageable list of stocks. Don't be afraid to experiment with different combinations of filters.

5. **Analyze the Results:** Once the screener returns a list of stocks, it's time to do your due diligence. Don't just blindly buy any stock that appears on the list. Research each company further to ensure it meets your investment criteria and risk tolerance.

6. **Backtesting (If Available):** If your screener offers backtesting capabilities, use it to test how your screening criteria would have performed historically. This can provide valuable insights into the effectiveness of your filters. However, remember that past performance is not indicative of future results.

7. **Save Your Screens:** Once you've created a set of filters that works well for you, save it so you can easily use it again in the future.

Examples of Screening Strategies:

- **Growth Stock Screener:** Filters for companies with high revenue growth, earnings growth, and ROE.
- **Value Stock Screener:** Filters for companies with low P/E ratios, P/B ratios, and high dividend yields.
- **Technical Breakout Screener:** Filters for stocks that have recently broken out above key resistance levels on high volume.

Effective Screening:

- **Be Specific:** Use precise criteria and avoid vague terms.
- **Combine Filters:** Use a combination of fundamental and technical filters to narrow down your search.
- **Don't Over-Filter:** Be careful not to over-filter your criteria, as you may miss out on potential opportunities.
- **Regularly Review Your Screens:** Market conditions change, so it's important to regularly review and adjust your screening criteria as needed.
- **Use Multiple Screeners:** Don't rely on just one screener. Try using different screeners to get a broader perspective.

Unlocking Trading Opportunities with Stock Screeners

Stock screeners are invaluable tools for any trader or investor. They empower you to efficiently filter through the vast sea of stocks and pinpoint those that align with your specific trading strategies and investment objectives. By mastering the art of using stock screeners, you can save time, enhance your research process, and significantly improve your chances of finding profitable trading opportunities. Remember, however, that screening is just the first step. Thorough due diligence and a well-defined trading plan are essential for long-term success.

Chapter 28: Decoding the Options Market: A Comprehensive Guide

Options trading offers a unique and powerful way to participate in the market, but it also comes with significant risks. This chapter will provide a comprehensive overview of options, explaining their mechanics, key concepts, and common strategies.

Part 1: Understanding the Basics of Options

Options are contracts that give the buyer the *right*, but not the *obligation*, to buy or sell an underlying asset (usually a stock) at a specific price (the strike price) on or before a specific date (the expiration date). The seller of the option has the *obligation* to fulfill the contract if the buyer chooses to exercise it.

Key Terminology:

- **Underlying Asset:** The stock or other asset that the option contract is based on.
- **Strike Price:** The price at which the underlying asset can be bought or sold if the option is exercised.
- **Expiration Date:** The date on which the option contract expires.
- **Premium:** The price paid by the buyer to the seller for the option contract.
- **Call Option:** Gives the buyer the right to *buy* the underlying asset.
- **Put Option:** Gives the buyer the right to *sell* the underlying asset.

In-the-Money (ITM), At-the-Money (ATM), and Out-of-the-Money (OTM):

- **ITM:** A call option is ITM when the underlying asset's price is *above* the strike price. A put option is ITM when the underlying asset's price is *below* the strike price.
- **ATM:** An option is ATM when the underlying asset's price is *equal to* the strike price.
- **OTM:** A call option is OTM when the underlying asset's price is *below* the strike price. A put option is OTM when the underlying asset's price is *above* the strike price.

Part 2: The Risks of Options Trading

Options offer unique advantages and disadvantages compared to simply buying or selling stocks.

Advantages:

- **Leverage:** Options provide leverage, allowing you to control a large number of shares with a relatively small investment (the premium). This can amplify potential gains, but also losses.
- **Flexibility:** Options can be used for a variety of strategies, including hedging (protecting existing stock positions), speculation (betting on the direction of the price), and income generation (selling covered calls or cash-secured puts).
- **Profit from Any Market Direction:** You can profit from rising, falling, or even sideways markets using different options strategies.

Disadvantages:

- **Time Decay (Theta):** Options are wasting assets. Their value erodes over time, especially as the expiration date approaches. This is known as time decay or theta.

- **Volatility Risk:** Option prices are highly sensitive to changes in volatility. Increased volatility can increase option prices, while decreased volatility can decrease option prices.

- **Complexity:** Options trading is more complex than stock trading. Understanding the various strategies and the Greeks requires significant study and practice.

- **Risk of Loss:** You can lose your entire premium if the option expires worthless.

Part 3: Understanding the Greeks: Measuring Option Sensitivity

The "Greeks" are a set of mathematical measures that quantify the sensitivity of an option's price to various factors. Understanding the Greeks is essential for managing risk and making informed trading decisions.

- **Delta (Δ):** Measures how much an option's price is expected to change for every $1 change in the underlying asset's price. Delta ranges from 0 to 1 for calls and 0 to -1 for puts.

- **Gamma (Γ):** Measures the rate of change of delta. It shows how much delta will change for every $1 change in the underlying asset's price.

- **Theta (Θ):** Measures how much an option's price is expected to decline as time passes (time decay).

- **Vega (ν):** Measures how much an option's price is expected to change for a 1% change in implied volatility.

- **Rho (ρ):** Measures how much an option's price is expected to change for a 1% change in interest rates. Rho is typically less important than the other Greeks.

How Traders Use the Greeks:

- **Risk Management:** The Greeks help traders assess and manage the various risks associated with options positions.

- **Portfolio Construction:** Understanding the Greeks allows traders to build diversified portfolios with specific risk and reward profiles.

- **Trading Strategies:** Many options strategies are based on managing the Greeks.

- **Option Pricing:** The Greeks are used in option pricing models (like the Black-Scholes model) to calculate the theoretical value of an option.

Important:

- **Dynamic Nature:** The Greeks are not static; they change constantly as the underlying asset's price, time to expiration, volatility, and interest rates change.

- **Estimates, Not Guarantees:** The Greeks provide estimates, not guarantees. Actual market movements can differ from the predictions based on the Greeks.

Part 4: Common Options Strategies

Covered Call: Selling call options against shares of stock you already own. This strategy generates income (the premium received) but limits your potential upside if the stock price rises significantly.

- **Protective Put:** Buying put options to protect your stock position from downside risk. This is like buying insurance for your stocks.

- **Long Call:** Buying call options in anticipation of the underlying asset's price rising. This strategy offers leveraged upside potential.

- **Long Put:** Buying put options in anticipation of the underlying asset's price falling. This strategy allows you to profit from a decline in the stock price.

- **Straddle:** Buying both a call and a put option with the same strike price and expiration date. This strategy profits from significant price movement in either direction

- **Strangle:** Buying both a call and a put option with different strike prices but the same expiration date. This strategy is similar to a straddle but requires a larger price movement to be profitable.

- **Spreads:** Involve buying and selling multiple options of the same type (calls or puts) with different strike prices or expiration dates. Spreads are used to limit risk and/or reduce the cost of the position. (Examples: Vertical spreads, Calendar spreads, Diagonal spreads)

Navigating the Complex World of Options

Options trading offers a powerful set of tools for traders and investors, but it's essential to understand the complexities and risks involved. By thoroughly studying options mechanics, understanding the Greeks, and practicing with different strategies, you can increase your chances of success in this challenging but potentially rewarding market. Remember, options trading is not for everyone. It requires knowledge, discipline, and a clear understanding of your own risk tolerance. Start small, learn continuously, and always manage your risk carefully.

Chapter 29: Catalysts: Igniting Stock Price Movement

Catalysts are the lifeblood of market movement, the sparks that ignite significant price changes. This extended chapter delves deeper into the intricacies of catalyst identification, analysis, and trading, providing a more comprehensive understanding of their role in the market. I personally don't take a trade unless it has 2-3 catalysts (reasons) that

Categorizing Catalysts: A Finer Grain:

While our previous categories are helpful, let's refine them for more precise analysis:

- Fundamental Catalysts: These relate to the core financial health and operations of a company. Earnings reports, revenue growth, profit margins, new product launches, changes in management, mergers and acquisitions, and divestitures fall under this category. These catalysts often have a longer-lasting impact on stock prices.

- Technical Catalysts: These stem from market dynamics and trading activity. Breakouts above key resistance levels, breakdowns below support levels, high trading volume, and changes in short interest can act as technical catalysts. These catalysts can be more short-term in nature.

- Sentiment-Driven Catalysts: These are driven by investor psychology and market perception. News headlines, analyst ratings, economic data releases, and even social media trends can influence investor sentiment and trigger price movements. These catalysts can be highly volatile and unpredictable.

- Event-Driven Catalysts: These are tied to specific events, such as regulatory approvals, legal decisions, clinical trial results, or geopolitical events. These catalysts can be binary in nature, with a clear positive or negative outcome.

Identifying and Analyzing Catalysts: Advanced Techniques:

- Deep Dive into Financial Statements: Don't just look at the headline numbers in earnings reports. Analyze the underlying details, such as revenue growth drivers, cost structure, and cash flow. Look for trends and compare the company's performance to its competitors.

- Scrutinize Company Presentations and Conference Calls: These events often provide valuable insights into management's strategy and outlook. Pay attention to the Q&A sessions, where analysts often ask probing questions.

- Follow Industry News and Trends: Stay informed about developments in the industry the company operates in. New technologies, changing consumer preferences, and regulatory changes can all have a significant impact on a company's prospects.

- Monitor Social Media and Online Forums: While you should be cautious about information from these sources, they can sometimes provide early indications of emerging trends or sentiment shifts. Look for discussions about specific companies or industries.

- Use Catalyst Calendars and News Aggregators: Several websites and platforms provide calendars of upcoming events, such as earnings releases, conferences, and economic data releases. News aggregators can help you stay on top of the latest news and developments.

- Consider the "Why" Behind the Move: Don't just focus on the news itself. Try to understand *why* the market is reacting the way it is. Is the news truly significant, or is the reaction overblown?

Trading Strategies Based on Catalysts: Advanced Concepts:

- Pre-Catalyst Trading: This strategy involves anticipating the market's reaction to an upcoming catalyst and taking a position beforehand. This requires careful analysis and a good understanding of the company and its industry.

- Post-Catalyst Trading: This strategy involves trading after a catalyst has been announced. Traders who use this approach often look for opportunities to capitalize on the market's reaction to the news.

- Volatility Trading: Catalysts often lead to increased volatility. Options traders can use strategies like straddles or strangles to profit from these price swings.

- Pairs Trading: This strategy involves taking a long position in one stock and a short position in another stock in the same industry, based on the expectation that one stock will outperform the other due to a catalyst.

Risk Management and Refinement: Advanced Considerations:

- Position Sizing Based on Catalyst Impact: The size of your position should depend not only on your risk tolerance but also on the potential impact of the catalyst. A more significant catalyst might warrant a larger position (within your risk limits), while a less significant catalyst might require a smaller position.

- Implied Volatility and Options Pricing: If you're trading options around a catalyst event, pay close attention to implied volatility. Implied volatility tends to increase before a catalyst and then decrease afterward. This can affect the pricing of options.

- Beware of "Buy the Rumor, Sell the News": Sometimes, the market will anticipate a catalyst, and the price of the stock will run up in advance. When the catalyst is finally announced, the price may actually decline as investors take profits.

- Consider the Time Horizon: Some catalysts have a short-term impact, while others have a longer-term impact. Your trading strategy should be aligned with your time horizon.

Example

A biotech company is awaiting FDA approval for a new drug. The market is anticipating a positive outcome, and the stock price has been steadily rising. However, you notice that short interest in the stock is also relatively high, suggesting that some investors are betting against the company. You also observe that the implied volatility of the company's options is elevated. Based on this information, you might consider a strategy that profits from either a positive or negative outcome, such as a long straddle.

Catalysts are the essential drivers of stock price movement. Mastering catalyst analysis and trading requires a deep understanding of financial analysis, market dynamics, and investor psychology. By combining fundamental analysis, technical analysis, and sentiment analysis, you can improve your ability to identify and capitalize on catalyst-driven opportunities. Remember that risk management is paramount, and continuous learning is essential for success in this dynamic field.

"Buy the Rumor, Sell the News": Deconstructing the Adage

This saying encapsulates a common market phenomenon: stock prices often react to anticipated events *before* they officially occur. Here's the logic:

1. **The Rumor Stage:** Whispers and speculation about a potential positive development (e.g., a new product launch, a successful clinical trial, a merger) begin to circulate. Traders, anticipating that the official news will boost the stock price, start buying shares. This increased demand drives the price up.

2. **The News Stage:** The anticipated news is finally released. At this point, many traders who bought on the rumor take their profits, selling their shares. This surge of selling pressure can cause the stock price to plateau, stabilize, or even decline, despite the positive news.

The core idea is to capitalize on the pre-news price run-up and then exit before the potential post-news sell-off.

Why Does This Happen?

Several factors contribute to this phenomenon:

- **Information Asymmetry:** Some traders may have earlier access to information or be better at interpreting subtle clues, giving them an edge in the rumor stage.

- **Speculation and Sentiment:** Rumors, even if unsubstantiated, can generate excitement and positive sentiment, attracting momentum traders and speculators.

- **Profit-Taking:** Traders who bought on the rumor are looking to capitalize on their gains. The news event provides a convenient opportunity to do so.

- **Market Expectations:** If the actual news is less impressive than what the market anticipated, it can lead to disappointment and selling pressure.

The Challenges and Risks:

While the "buy the rumor, sell the news" strategy sounds simple, it's fraught with challenges and risks:

- **Rumor Verification:** Distinguishing credible rumors from baseless speculation is difficult. Acting on false information can lead to significant losses.

- **Timing:** Accurately timing the entry and exit points is crucial. Getting in too late or staying in too long can be detrimental.

- **Volatility:** News-driven trades can be highly volatile, with rapid price swings. This requires careful risk management and the ability to handle emotional pressure.

- **News Interpretation:** The market's reaction to news can be unpredictable. Even positive news can sometimes lead to a price decline if it doesn't meet high expectations.

- **Competition:** News trading is highly competitive, especially with the rise of algorithmic trading and sophisticated institutional investors.

News Trading: A Broader Perspective

"Buy the rumor, sell the news" is just one aspect of news trading. Many traders focus on analyzing news events and their potential impact on stock prices. This requires:

- **Fundamental Analysis:** Understanding the underlying business, industry, and economic factors that can be affected by the news.

- **Technical Analysis:** Using charts and technical indicators to identify potential entry and exit points.

- **Speed and Technology:** Getting access to news quickly and having the tools to execute trades rapidly is essential. This is where specialized news feeds, financial data platforms, and trading software come into play.

- **Discipline and Patience:** News trading requires discipline to stick to a trading plan and avoid emotional reactions. Patience is also important, as not every news event will create a profitable trading opportunity.

Volatility: The Constant Companion

One thing is certain: news events often create volatility. This volatility can be a double-edged sword. It presents opportunities for quick profits but also carries the risk of substantial losses. Whether you're trying to "buy the rumor, sell the news" or simply react to news events, understanding and managing volatility is paramount.

Chapter 30: Mastering Trading Strategies: A Practical Guide

This chapter explores a variety of trading strategies, ranging from short-term scalping to longer-term option strategies and swing trading approaches. It emphasizes the importance of finding a trading style that matches your personality and risk tolerance.

Short-Term Strategies: Scalping and Day Trading

1. The MACD 10% Scalp Play:

This strategy aims to capture small, quick profits by focusing on range breakouts and retracements.

- **Key Factors:**
    - **Range Consolidation:** Identify a period of compressed price action and a flat MACD (3-15 minutes).
    - **Range Breakout & MACD Expansion:** Observe a break of the range accompanied by expansion of the MACD lines.
    - **Retracement & Entry:** Look for a price retracement and wait for the Fast MACD to cross back above the Slow MACD while both are above the zero line. Enter long (or short for a short scalp).
    - **Stop-Loss:** Place a hard stop 0.02 below the retracement low (or high for short).
    - **Exit:** Exit the position when the Fast MACD crosses back below (or above for short) the Slow MACD.
- **Setups:**
    - Gap out of range
    - Volatility within range
    - Trending day
    - Failed breakdown
    - Gap down into key support
    - Day 2 following intraday reversal

Part 2: Options Strategies

1. Put Credit Spread:

A bullish strategy that generates income by selling put options.

- **Mechanics:** Sell a put option with a higher strike price and buy a put option with a lower strike price, both with the same expiration date.
- **Goal:** Profit if the underlying stock price stays above the higher strike price.
- **Maximum Profit:** The net credit received when opening the position.

- **Maximum Loss:** The difference between the strike prices, minus the net credit received.

- **Break Even Point:** Higher strike price minus the net credit received.

2. Call Credit Spread:
A bearish strategy that generates income by selling call options.

- **Mechanics:** Sell a call option with a lower strike price and buy a call option with a higher strike price, both with the same expiration date.

- **Goal:** Profit if the underlying stock price stays below the lower strike price.

- **Maximum Profit:** The net credit received when opening the position.

- **Maximum Loss:** The difference between the strike prices, minus the net credit received.

- **Breakeven Point:** Lower strike price plus the net credit received.

3. Covered Call:
A bullish strategy that generates income by selling call options against shares of stock you already own.

- **Mechanics:** Own 100 shares of stock and sell one call option contract.
- **Goal:** Generate income from the premium received.
- **Maximum Profit:** (Strike Price - Purchase Price) * 100 + Premium Received
- **Maximum Loss:** (Purchase Price - $0) * 100 - Premium Received
- **Break Even Point:** Purchase Price - (Premium Received / 100)

You decide to sell one covered call option contract (representing 100 shares) with a strike price of $55 and an expiration date three months out. The premium you receive for selling this call option is $2 per share, or $200 total (100 shares x $2 premium).

Possible Outcomes:

- Scenario 1: Stock Price Stays Below $55 at Expiration: Let's say XYZ stock price is $53 at the option's expiration. The call option expires worthless, meaning the buyer will not exercise their right to purchase your shares at $55. You keep the $200 premium, and you still own your 100 shares of XYZ stock, now worth $5,300. Your total profit for the period is the $200 premium.

- Scenario 2: Stock Price Rises Above $55 at Expiration: Let's say XYZ stock price is $57 at expiration. The call option is now "in the money," and the buyer will likely exercise their right to buy your 100 shares at $55. You are obligated to sell your shares at $55, receiving $5,500. You made $500 on the sale of the shares (100 shares x $5 profit per share). Add the $200 premium and your total profit is $700. You no longer own the shares, but you have the cash.

- Scenario 3: Stock Price Rises Significantly Above $55: Let's say XYZ stock price jumps to $60 at expiration. The call option is deep in the money, and the buyer will definitely exercise it. You're still obligated to sell your shares at $55, receiving $5,500. You miss out on the additional $5 per share gain above the strike price (100 shares x $5 = $500) that you would have had if you had not sold the call. You still made $700 from the covered call (the $500 profit on the shares up to the strike price plus the $200 premium). This scenario illustrates the opportunity cost of selling a covered call. Your profit is capped at the strike price plus the premium received.

- Scenario 4: Stock Price Falls: Let's say XYZ stock price falls to $48 at expiration. The call option expires worthless, which is good for you (you keep the premium). However, your 100 shares are now worth $4,800, a loss of $200 from their initial value. You've offset some of that loss with the $200 premium you received, but you're still down overall. Covered calls do not protect your shares from losses if the price declines.

Key Points:

- Covered calls are designed to generate income (the premium) from shares you already own.
- Your profit is capped at the strike price of the call option plus the premium received.
- Covered calls do *not* protect your shares from losses if the stock price declines. You still participate in any price drop of the stock.
- Selling covered calls makes the most sense when you expect the stock price to remain relatively stable or rise only moderately.

4. The Wheel Strategy:

A strategy that combines selling cash-secured puts and covered calls to generate income and potentially acquire shares at a discount.

- **Mechanics:** Sell cash-secured puts until assigned shares. Then, sell covered calls on the shares until they are called away. Repeat the cycle.
- **Goal:** Generate income and potentially acquire shares at a discounted price.

Part 3: Swing Trading Strategies

Swing trading aims to capture short-to-medium-term price swings.

1. Trend Following:

Capitalizing on established trends.

- **Mechanics:** Identify uptrends (using moving averages, trendlines, etc.) and buy. Identify downtrends and sell short.
- **Entry:** After confirmation of the trend.
- **Exit:** When the trend shows signs of weakening.

2. Breakout Trading:

Entering trades after a price breaks through a key support or resistance level.

- **Mechanics:** Identify key levels. Buy after a break above resistance. Sell short after a break below support.
- **Confirmation:** Look for increased volume during the breakout.
- **Stop-Loss:** Essential to limit losses from false breakouts.

3. Pullback Trading:

Entering trades after a temporary price pullback within a larger trend.

- **Mechanics:** Identify an established trend. Wait for a pullback. Enter near a support level (for uptrends) or resistance level (for downtrends).

4. Chart Pattern Recognition:
Identifying and trading based on chart patterns (flags, pennants, triangles, etc.).

- **Mechanics:** Learn to recognize common chart patterns. Enter trades based on the pattern's implications.

5. Moving Average Crossovers:
Using moving average crossovers as trading signals.

- **Mechanics:** Use a combination of short-term and long-term moving averages. Buy when the short-term MA crosses above the long-term MA. Sell when the short-term MA crosses below the long-term MA.

Part 4: Correlated Assets Trading (The Tandem Trade)
This strategy involves identifying and exploiting correlated assets.

- **Mechanics:** Research and identify assets with a strong historical correlation (e.g., BOIL and KOLD). Capitalize on their interconnected movements.

Part 5: Finding Your Trading Style
Your trading style should align with your personality, risk tolerance, and available time. It may evolve over time as you gain experience. Mastering a specific trading style is crucial for long-term success.

Chapter 31: Learning from the Masters: Investing Wisdom and Timeless Classics

This chapter explores the wisdom of renowned investors and highlights key insights from influential investing books. It's not just about name-dropping; it's about extracting actionable lessons that you can apply to your own trading and investing journey.

Part 1: Giants of Investing: Their Wisdom and Strategies

Instead of just listing names, let's focus on specific lessons and strategies from each investor.

- Warren Buffett:
  - Value Investing: Focus on undervalued companies with strong fundamentals, a "moat" (competitive advantage), and excellent management.
  - Long-Term Perspective: Invest for the long haul, not for short-term gains. "Be fearful when others are greedy, and greedy when others are fearful."
  - Circle of Competence: Invest only in businesses you understand.
- Ray Dalio:
  - Macroeconomic Analysis: Understand global economic trends and market cycles.
  - Principles-Based Investing: Develop a set of principles to guide your decision-making. Transparency and idea meritocracy.
  - Data-Driven Approach: Use data and analysis to back up your investment decisions.
- Carl Icahn:
  - Activist Investing: Take an active role in companies you invest in, pushing for changes that increase shareholder value.
  - Focus on Undervalued Assets: Identify companies with hidden value that the market has overlooked.
  - Aggressive Approach: Don't be afraid to take calculated risks.
- Robert F. Smith:
  - Focus on Technology: Invest in disruptive technologies with high growth potential.
  - Private Equity: Invest in private companies and leverage operational expertise to drive value creation.
  - Philanthropy: Give back to the community and use your success to make a positive impact.
- Cathie Wood:
  - Disruptive Innovation: Invest in companies at the forefront of technological innovation.

○ Long-Term Growth: Focus on long-term growth potential rather than short-term market fluctuations.

○ High-Conviction Investing: Have strong conviction in your investment ideas.

● Jeff Bezos:

○ Customer Obsession: Focus on delivering exceptional value to customers.

○ Long-Term Vision: Think long-term and don't be afraid to disrupt existing industries.

○ Relentless Innovation: Continuously innovate and experiment.

Part 2: Timeless Investing Classics: A Curated Reading List

Instead of just listing the books, let's highlight the *key takeaways* from each one.

● The Intelligent Investor by Benjamin Graham:

○ Margin of Safety: Buy assets at a significant discount to their intrinsic value.

○ Value Investing: Focus on fundamental analysis and long-term investing.

○ Mr. Market: Don't let emotions influence your investment decisions.

● Security Analysis by Benjamin Graham & David Dodd:

○ Fundamental Analysis: A deep dive into analyzing financial statements and assessing a company's intrinsic value.

○ Thorough Research: Emphasizes the importance of rigorous research and due diligence.

● One Up On Wall Street by Peter Lynch:

○ Invest in What You Know: Focus on companies and industries you understand.

○ Long-Term Perspective: Don't try to time the market.

○ "Ten Baggers": Look for companies with the potential to grow many times in value.

● The Little Book That Still Beats the Market by Joel Greenblatt:

○ Magic Formula: A simple yet effective formula for identifying undervalued companies based on earnings yield and return on capital.

● The Essays of Warren Buffett: Lessons for Corporate America:

○ Value Investing: A collection of Buffett's writings on value investing, business principles, and long-term investing.

● Market Wizards by Jack D. Schwager:

○ Trading Psychology: Interviews with top traders reveal their strategies, mindsets, and experiences.

- Reminiscences of a Stock Operator by Edwin Lefèvre:

○ Market Psychology: A classic novel that explores the psychology of trading and the pitfalls that can derail even experienced traders.

- Trading in the Zone by Mark Douglas:

○ Trading Psychology: Focuses on the psychological aspects of trading, emphasizing the importance of emotional discipline and risk management. *This book had a significant impact on your trading journey, as it helped you understand the importance of mindset and consistent execution.*

- The Disciplined Trader by Mark Douglas:

○ Trading Psychology: Explores how traders can improve their decision-making by understanding the mental and emotional factors that influence their trading.

- Think and Grow Rich by Napoleon Hill:

○ Mindset for Success: While not strictly about investing, this book explores the principles of success and personal development, which are highly relevant to achieving financial goals.

Part 3: Actionable Takeaways and Integrating the Wisdom

- Identify Your Trading Style: Which of these investors and books resonate most with you? Do you prefer value investing, growth investing, technical analysis, or a combination?

- Develop a Trading Plan: Based on your chosen style, create a detailed trading plan that outlines your entry and exit rules, risk management strategy, and position sizing.

- Continuous Learning: The market is constantly evolving. Commit to continuous learning by reading books, following market news, and analyzing your own performance.

- Practice and Patience: Don't expect to become a successful investor overnight. It takes time, practice, and patience to develop your skills and refine your approach.

Your Personal Experience:

Your experience with "Trading in the Zone" is a great example of how a book can have a profound impact on your trading journey. Highlight how the book helped you understand the importance of mindset and discipline, and how it led you to explore swing trading strategies.

Conclusion: Building Your Investing Foundation

Learning from the masters is an essential part of becoming a successful investor. By studying the wisdom of these giants and immersing yourself in these timeless classics, you can build a solid foundation for your own investing journey. Remember, it's not just about what you learn, but how you *apply* that knowledge to your own trading and investment decisions.

MARKET
SYMPHONY
A MUSICIAN'S GUIDE TO TRADING
STOCKS, ETFS, AND DIGITAL ASSETS

Chapter 32: Key Lessons for Trading Success: Mindset, Community, and Continuous Learning

This chapter delves into the crucial lessons that underpin successful trading, emphasizing the symbiotic relationship between a robust mindset, a supportive community, and a commitment to continuous learning. These elements are not merely supplementary; they are foundational pillars upon which a sustainable and profitable trading career is built.

The Power of Community: Learning and Growing Together

Trading, while often an individual pursuit, thrives in a collaborative environment. Connecting with other traders is more than just networking; it's about forging a community of shared learning, mutual support, and collective growth.

- **Shared Experiences: The Human Element:** Trading can be emotionally taxing. The rollercoaster of wins and losses, the constant uncertainty, and the pressure to perform can take a toll. Sharing these experiences – both the highs and the lows – with others who understand the unique pressures of the market is vital for emotional resilience. It normalizes the emotional challenges and provides a safe space to discuss anxieties, frustrations, and triumphs.

- **Diverse Perspectives: Broadening Your Horizons:** The market is a multifaceted beast, viewed through countless lenses. Engaging with other traders exposes you to diverse trading styles, strategies, and analytical approaches. You might encounter a scalper who thrives on short-term price fluctuations, a value investor who patiently seeks undervalued companies, or a technical analyst who deciphers chart patterns. This exposure broadens your understanding of the market's complexities and challenges your own assumptions.

- **Accelerated Learning: Standing on the Shoulders of Giants:** Learning from others' mistakes – and, of course, their successes – is a shortcut to wisdom. Hearing about another trader's disastrous trade can be a powerful lesson in risk management, far more impactful than simply reading about it in a book. Conversely, analyzing a successful trade can illuminate new strategies and refine your own approach. The collective knowledge of a community can significantly accelerate your learning curve.

- **Emotional Support: A Buffer Against Volatility:** Market volatility can trigger fear, greed, and panic, leading to impulsive decisions. A supportive community acts as a buffer against these emotional swings. When you're struggling, having someone to talk to who understands the emotional rollercoaster of trading can be invaluable. They can offer encouragement, perspective, and practical advice, reminding you of your trading plan and helping you avoid rash actions.

How to Find Your Tribe:

- **Online Forums and Trading Groups:** These platforms offer a convenient way to connect with traders from around the world. They are hubs for sharing ideas, asking questions, discussing market trends, and debating different strategies. Be selective and find communities that align with your trading style and values.

- **Local Meetups:** Connecting with traders in person adds a deeper dimension to community building. Local meetups foster a stronger sense of camaraderie and allow for more nuanced, in-depth discussions.

- **Social Media (with Caution):** Platforms like Twitter and LinkedIn can be used to connect with traders and follow market commentators. However, exercise caution and be discerning about the information you consume. Many "gurus" and "influencers" prioritize self-promotion over genuine insights.

- **Mentorship Programs:** Seeking out a formal mentorship program can provide structured guidance and support from experienced traders.

Key Principles for Community Engagement:

- **Active Participation:** Don't be a passive observer. Ask questions, share your insights, offer constructive criticism, and contribute to the conversation.

- **Focus on the Fundamentals:** While discussing specific trades can be helpful, don't get lost in the noise. Focus on core principles like trading psychology, risk management, position sizing, and the importance of a well-defined trading plan.

- **Give Back:** As you gain experience and knowledge, consider mentoring newer traders. Sharing your insights not only benefits others but also solidifies your own understanding of the market.

- **Be Discerning:** Not all advice is created equal. Be wary of "gurus" promising guaranteed riches or "hot tips" without sound reasoning. Always do your own research and verify information from multiple sources.

Part 2: The Importance of Mentorship and Guidance

While community is crucial, personalized guidance can significantly accelerate your progress. Seeking a mentor or trading coach can provide invaluable support and expertise.

- **Personalized Feedback: Tailored to Your Needs:** A mentor can provide specific feedback on your trading plan, strategy, and execution. They can identify blind spots in your analysis, point out areas for improvement, and offer tailored advice based on your individual strengths and weaknesses.

- **Experience and Insights: Learning from the Trenches:** Mentors bring years of experience and a wealth of market knowledge. They can share insights that aren't found in books, offering practical wisdom gleaned from navigating market cycles and overcoming challenges.

- **Accountability: Staying on Track:** A mentor can provide accountability, helping you stay disciplined and stick to your trading plan, even when it's tempting to deviate. Knowing that you have to discuss your trades with someone can deter impulsive decisions and encourage consistent execution.

- **Faster Progress: Avoiding Costly Mistakes:** By learning from someone who has already made (and learned from) their share of mistakes, you can avoid many common pitfalls and accelerate your development as a trader.

How to Find a Mentor:

- **Networking:** Attend local trading meetups, connect with traders online, and reach out to those whose experience and expertise you admire.

- **Online Platforms:** Some platforms specialize in connecting traders with mentors or coaches.

- **Trading Schools and Courses:** Many offer mentorship programs as part of their curriculum.

Part 3: Research Your Research: Due Diligence and Critical Thinking

In the age of readily available information, it's easy to get overwhelmed with data and opinions. Developing strong research skills and critical thinking abilities is essential for navigating this information overload and making informed trading decisions.

- **Question Everything: The Skeptical Investor:** Don't take anything at face value. Be skeptical of "hot tips," market predictions, and even your own biases. Always verify information from multiple reputable sources.

- **Develop Your Own Analysis: Beyond the Headlines:** Don't rely solely on others' analysis. Learn to conduct your own technical and fundamental analysis. Develop the ability to interpret financial statements, analyze charts, and understand market dynamics.

- **Understand the "Why": The Power of Rationale:** Don't just focus on *what* to trade; understand *why* a trade makes sense. What are the underlying factors driving the price movement? What is the risk-reward profile? Developing a strong rationale for each trade is crucial for consistent decision-making.

- **Be Independent: Charting Your Own Course:** While community and mentorship are valuable, ultimately, you are responsible for your own trading decisions. Use the insights and knowledge you gain from others as resources, but develop the confidence to think independently and chart your own course.

Part 4: Key Mindset Principles for Successful Trading

Mindset is paramount in trading. Developing the right mental framework is just as important as mastering technical or fundamental analysis.

- **Don't Marry Stocks: Detachment and Objectivity:** Avoid emotional attachment to any stock, company, or investment idea. Be objective and willing to sell when your trading plan dictates, even if you have a personal affinity for the company. Remember, you're trading a ticker symbol, not a marriage.

- **This is Not Gambling; You are the Casino: Managing Probabilities:** Successful trading is about managing probabilities and having a long-term edge. It's not about luck or chasing quick wins. Like a casino, you need to understand the odds, manage risk effectively, and have a robust risk management plan. Individual trades are like individual hands of poker; you might lose some, but the goal is to win in the long run.

- **Patience and Discipline: The Power of Waiting:** The market rewards patience and punishes impulsiveness. Wait for the right opportunities that align with your trading plan. Avoid chasing trades or making emotional decisions driven by fear or greed.

- **Emotional Control: Mastering Your Inner Self:** Fear and greed are powerful emotions that can cloud judgment and lead to costly mistakes. Learn to manage your emotions and avoid letting them dictate your trading decisions. Develop strategies for staying calm and focused, even during periods of market volatility.

- **Continuous Learning: The Ever-Evolving Market:** The market is a dynamic, ever-evolving entity. Commit to lifelong learning and adaptation. Stay updated on market trends, economic data, and new trading strategies. Be willing to acknowledge your mistakes and learn from them.

- **Personal Growth: Beyond the Profits:** Trading is not just about making money; it's about personal growth. It's about developing valuable skills like discipline, patience, analytical thinking, and emotional resilience. These skills are transferable and can benefit you in all aspects of life.

Part 5: The Importance of a Trading Plan and Journaling

Two essential tools for trading success are a well-defined trading plan and a detailed trading journal.

- **Trading Plan: Your Roadmap to Success:** A comprehensive trading plan is your roadmap for navigating the market. It outlines your investment objectives, risk tolerance, trading strategies, entry and exit rules, position sizing, and risk management protocols. It provides a framework for making consistent and disciplined decisions, preventing impulsive actions and emotional trading.

- **Trading Journal: Reflecting and Refining:** A trading journal is your personal record of your trading activity. Document each trade, including your rationale, entry and exit points, position size, risk assessment

TRIANGLE
ROYALTY GROUP

Chapter 33: The Future of Trading: Navigating the Age of AI

The rise of Artificial Intelligence (AI) is no longer a futuristic fantasy; it's a present reality reshaping industries globally, and the world of trading is no exception. AI's potential to revolutionize how we interact with financial markets is immense, comparable to the impact of the printing press on communication. This chapter explores the evolving landscape of AI-driven trading, examining its potential, limitations, and the crucial role of human traders in this new era.

AI: A Powerful Tool, Not a Replacement

The question isn't *if* AI will impact trading, but *how*. While some envision a fully automated future where algorithms reign supreme, a more nuanced perspective recognizes AI as a powerful *tool* that augments, rather than replaces, human capabilities. Just as a skilled carpenter uses a variety of tools to build a house, successful traders in the age of AI must learn to effectively integrate AI into their workflow.

Strengths and Limitations of AI in Trading

AI excels at tasks that are challenging for humans:

- **Data Processing:** AI can analyze massive datasets far beyond human capacity, identifying subtle patterns and correlations that would be invisible to the naked eye.
- **Pattern Recognition:** AI algorithms can detect complex patterns in market data, potentially predicting price movements with greater accuracy than traditional methods.
- **Speed and Precision:** AI can execute trades at lightning speed, capitalizing on fleeting opportunities and minimizing slippage.
- **Real-Time Optimization:** AI can dynamically adjust trading strategies in response to changing market conditions.

However, AI also has significant limitations:

- **Lack of Human Intuition:** AI, in its current form, lacks the intuition, emotional intelligence, and common sense that humans possess. It struggles to understand the nuances of human behavior, which plays a crucial role in market dynamics.
- **Inability to Adapt to the Truly Unforeseen:** AI models are trained on historical data. They may struggle to adapt to truly novel events or "black swan" occurrences that fall outside their training parameters. Human judgment and adaptability are essential in these situations.
- **Overfitting and Bias:** AI models can be prone to overfitting, where they become too specialized to the training data and perform poorly in real-world scenarios. They can also inherent biases present in the data, leading to skewed or inaccurate predictions.
- **Explainability and Transparency:** The "black box" nature of some AI algorithms can make it difficult to understand how they arrive at their decisions. This lack of transparency can be problematic, especially in regulated industries.

The Human Element: The Indispensable Factor

Financial markets are not purely rational systems; they are deeply influenced by human psychology, sentiment, and unpredictable events. Fear and greed, those age-old drivers of market behavior, continue to exert a profound influence on price movements. AI, despite its sophistication, struggles to fully comprehend these irrational yet powerful forces.

The complexity of global markets further underscores the importance of the human element. Consider the immense capital flows, the intricate network of interconnected institutions, and the influence of geopolitical events, human psychology, and seemingly random "black swan" events. These factors create a dynamic and unpredictable environment where human judgment, adaptability, and critical thinking remain invaluable.

The Human-in-the-Loop: The Future of Trading

The future of trading will likely be characterized by a symbiotic relationship between humans and AI. A "human-in-the-loop" approach, where traders effectively leverage AI tools while simultaneously maintaining a deep understanding of market dynamics, human behavior, and the limitations of AI, will be essential.

Traders who can:

- **Critically evaluate AI output:** Understand the limitations of AI algorithms and critically assess their recommendations.
- **Integrate AI insights with human judgment:** Combine AI-driven insights with their own market knowledge and intuition to make informed decisions.
- **Adapt to changing market conditions:** Recognize when AI models are no longer performing effectively and adjust their strategies accordingly.
- **Understand the ethical implications of AI:** Be aware of the potential biases and unintended consequences of using AI in trading.

...will gain a significant competitive advantage.

The Democratization of Trading: Empowering Individual Investors

AI has the potential to democratize trading by making sophisticated tools and insights more accessible to individual investors. AI-powered platforms could provide retail traders with access to:

- **Advanced analytics:** Tools for analyzing market data, identifying trends, and assessing risk.
- **Personalized trading strategies:** AI-driven recommendations tailored to individual risk tolerance and investment goals.
- **Automated trading execution:** Algorithms that can execute trades on behalf of individual investors.

This democratization could level the playing field and empower individuals to participate more effectively in the financial markets.

The Ongoing Evolution: Embracing Change and Adapting

The future of trading is not a static destination; it's a journey of continuous evolution. AI is just one of the many forces that will shape the markets in the years to come. As traders, we must:

- **Embrace change:** Be open to new technologies and adapt to the evolving market landscape.

- **Continuously refine our skills:** Develop the skills necessary to effectively leverage AI tools and integrate them into our trading strategies.

- **Focus on critical thinking and adaptability:** These human skills will become even more important in the age of AI.

A Collaborative Future for Humans and AI

AI is not a threat to human traders; it's a powerful tool that can enhance our abilities and open up new possibilities. The future of trading will be defined by a collaborative partnership between humans and AI, where human intuition and judgment are combined with the analytical power and speed of AI. By embracing these changes, adapting to new technologies, and continuously refining our skills, we can thrive in this dynamic and exciting new era of trading.

Chapter 34: Your Personal Toolbox: Building Your Financial House

This book has provided you with a collection of tools designed to help you build your financial house. It's no coincidence that the three most frequently used words throughout these pages are *risk*, *discipline*, and *plan*. If someone were to ask me the essential ingredients for trading success, those three words would be my unwavering response. They are the cornerstones upon which any profitable trading strategy is constructed.

A few years ago, I encountered a fascinating account of traders who selected stocks by throwing darts at a newspaper and even using Scrabble letters to generate stock tickers. While seemingly random, their approach revealed a powerful truth: the specific stock being traded is secondary to the *process* and *discipline* employed. These traders, despite their unconventional stock selection method, reportedly achieved an 80% success rate.

This anecdote underscores a crucial point: with the right *plan*, anyone can achieve trading success. The key is having a defined set of tools and strategies that are consistently applied. This book has offered you a diverse selection of such tools, allowing you to experiment and discover the perfect combination that resonates with your personality, risk tolerance, and trading style. Think of it as assembling a custom toolbox, carefully selecting the instruments that feel most comfortable and effective in your hands.

The Plan: The Foundation of Your Financial House

Your trading plan is the foundation upon which your entire financial house is built. It's not a whimsical document that changes with every market fluctuation or emotional impulse. It's a carefully crafted blueprint that outlines your trading goals, risk management rules, entry and exit strategies, and the specific tools you'll use to execute your plan. A constantly shifting foundation will inevitably lead to instability and eventual collapse.

The 50/50 Reality of the First Trade (and Beyond)

It's crucial to understand that your first trade after implementing your plan has a roughly 50/50 chance of success. While thorough research can tilt the odds slightly in your favor, the inherent uncertainty of the market means that any individual trade can be a winner or a loser. Don't let the outcome of a single trade, or even a handful of trades, dictate your overall strategy. A well-defined plan is designed to be followed *consistently* over a significant number of trades.

The Importance of a Statistical Sample:

Think of it like a baseball player. A single at-bat doesn't define their batting average. It's the cumulative performance over hundreds of at-bats that provides a true measure of their skill. Similarly, in trading, you need a *decent sample size* of trades to accurately assess the effectiveness of your strategy. Don't abandon your plan after a few losing trades. Give it time to play out, track your results meticulously, and make adjustments as needed.

The Power of Iteration and Refinement:

Your trading plan is not set in stone. It's a living document that should be reviewed and refined periodically. As you gain experience and gather more data, you'll likely discover areas where your plan can be improved. Don't be afraid to make changes, but always do so thoughtfully and based on objective analysis, not emotional reactions.

Building Your Personalized Toolbox:

This book has equipped you with a variety of tools, including:

- **Technical Analysis:** Chart patterns, indicators, trendlines – these are the tools you use to analyze price action and identify trading opportunities.

- **Fundamental Analysis:** Understanding financial statements, industry trends, and economic data – these tools help you assess the long-term value of your investments.

- **Risk Management:** Stop-loss orders, position sizing, diversification – these are the tools you use to protect your capital and manage risk.

- **Discipline and Emotional Control:** These are the internal tools that enable you to stick to your plan and avoid impulsive decisions.

The process of building your personalized toolbox involves experimentation and self-discovery. Try different tools, see what works best for you, and gradually refine your approach. There's no one-size-fits-all solution. The key is to find the combination of tools that aligns with your individual strengths and preferences.

Trading success is not about luck or intuition. It's about having a well-defined plan, a solid set of tools, and the discipline to execute your plan consistently. This book has provided you with the knowledge and tools you need to build your financial house. Now it's up to you to put them into practice, refine your approach, and build a successful trading career. Remember, trading is a journey, not a destination. Embrace the learning process, be patient, and never stop refining your toolbox.

MARKET SYMPHONY:
A Musician's Guide to
Trading Stocks, ETFs,
and Digital Assets

Chapter 35: Trading the Sidelines and Living the Dream (Almost)

Congratulations! You've reached the culmination of this introductory exploration into the fascinating and often challenging world of technical analysis and stock market trading. This book, hopefully, has served as a compass, providing direction and foundational knowledge for your journey into the markets. But remember, this is not the final destination; it's merely the launchpad. The real journey, the path to mastery, is a continuous process of learning, adapting, and evolving.

The financial landscape is in constant flux. Market dynamics shift with the tides of global events, new technologies disrupt established industries, and even the psychology of market participants ebbs and flows like the ocean. The knowledge you've gained from these pages is a powerful toolkit, but its effectiveness depends entirely on your ability to wield it skillfully, to refine it through experience, and to continuously expand upon it. Don't view this book as the ultimate authority, the definitive guide to trading success. Instead, see it as a stepping stone, a foundational framework upon which you will build your own unique trading approach.

The Unending Quest for Knowledge:

The pursuit of trading mastery is a lifelong endeavor, a continuous quest for knowledge. The market is a vast and complex organism, a living, breathing entity with its own rhythms and moods. There will always be more to learn, new strategies to explore, and unforeseen challenges to overcome. Embrace this continuous learning process. Cultivate an insatiable curiosity, a hunger for knowledge that drives you to constantly seek improvement. Devour books on trading, delve into market analysis reports, engage in thoughtful discussions with other traders, and, perhaps most importantly, meticulously analyze your own trades, both the winners and, especially, the losers. Don't just passively read; actively engage with the material. Question assumptions, challenge conventional wisdom, and form your own informed opinions.

Self-Awareness: The Cornerstone of Emotional Control:

One of the most valuable, and often overlooked, lessons in trading is self-awareness. The market can be an emotional crucible, testing your psychological resilience in ways you never imagined. Understanding your own biases, your emotional triggers, is paramount to making rational trading decisions. Are you susceptible to the fear of missing out (FOMO), leading you to chase overvalued stocks? Or are you prone to panic selling at the first sign of a market downturn? Do you let greed cloud your judgment, causing you to hold onto losing positions for too long? Identifying these emotional tendencies, acknowledging their influence, is the crucial first step towards controlling them and preventing them from sabotaging your trading performance. Keep a detailed trading journal, not just of your trades, but also of your emotional state during each trade. This will help you identify patterns in your emotional responses and develop strategies for managing them effectively. Consider practicing mindfulness or meditation to improve your emotional regulation.

Forging Your Trading Identity:

This brings us back to the central theme of this book: helping you discover your own trading style, the type of trader you are meant to be. Are you drawn to the fast-paced action of day trading, scalping small profits from intraday price fluctuations? Or do you prefer the more deliberate approach of swing trading, capturing short-to-medium term price movements? Perhaps you're more aligned with long-term investing, focusing on fundamental analysis and holding positions for years, patiently waiting for value to unfold. There is no single "correct" path. The optimal approach is the one that resonates with your individual personality, your risk tolerance, your available time commitment, and your long-term financial goals. Experiment with different approaches in a simulated environment or with small amounts of capital. Track your performance meticulously and analyze what works best for you. Don't be afraid to adapt your style as you gain experience and learn more about yourself.

The Long and Winding Road to Profitability:

The journey to consistent profitability is not a sprint; it's a marathon, a long and winding road with its fair share of potholes and detours. There will be setbacks, there will be losses, and there will be moments when you question your abilities and your chosen path. Don't let these inevitable challenges discourage you. Every successful trader, from the novice just starting out to the seasoned professional, has faced adversity. The defining characteristic of successful traders is not that they avoid losses, but that they learn from their mistakes, adapt their strategies, and persevere through difficult times. Analyze your losses meticulously. What went wrong? What could you have done differently? Use your mistakes as learning opportunities.

From Sports Cards to Stocks: Timeless Principles, Evolving Landscape:

Remember the analogy of your childhood sports card trading days. Just as you learned to assess the value of each card, to understand market trends (who was hot, who was not), and to negotiate effectively with other collectors, you must now apply those same fundamental principles to the stock market. It's about recognizing value, identifying opportunities where the market has mispriced an asset, and managing risk effectively to protect your capital. The scale is larger, the stakes are higher, but the underlying principles remain the same. However, the market landscape is constantly evolving. New technologies, new regulations, and new market participants are constantly changing the dynamics of the game. You must be willing to adapt your strategies and learn new skills to stay ahead of the curve.

Guiding Principles for the Ongoing Journey:

As you continue your trading education and begin to put your knowledge into practice, keep these essential principles at the forefront of your mind:

- **Relentless Learning:** Never stop learning. The market is a dynamic environment, and you must constantly adapt and evolve. Read books, follow market news, attend webinars, and engage with other traders.

- **Deep Self-Awareness:** Understand your own biases and emotional triggers. Learn to manage your emotions and avoid impulsive decisions. Practice mindfulness and emotional regulation techniques.

- **Unwavering Discipline:** Stick to your trading plan and avoid deviating based on emotions or external pressures. Develop a disciplined approach to risk management and trade execution.

- **Robust Risk Management:** Protect your capital by using stop-loss orders, position sizing, and diversification. Never risk more than you can afford to lose. Understand the different types of risk and how to mitigate them.

- **Patient Persistence:** Wait for the right opportunities and don't chase trades. Be patient and persistent in your pursuit of your trading goals.

- **Adaptable Strategies:** Be willing to adjust your strategies as market conditions change. The market is constantly evolving, and you must be able to adapt to stay ahead of the curve.

- **Humble Perspective:** Acknowledge that you don't have all the answers and be open to learning from your mistakes. Maintain a humble perspective and avoid overconfidence.

The Reality of Trading: Managing Expectations:

Let's be honest, none of us are overnight millionaires. This isn't about flipping burgers on Wall Street, getting rich quick, and retiring to a life of luxury (at least not immediately). This is about building a sustainable, potentially life-changing side hustle, one carefully executed trade at a time. It's about finding a harmonious balance between the exhilarating thrill of the chase and the serenity of a well-diversified portfolio. It's about setting realistic expectations and focusing on consistent, incremental progress.

The Emotional Crucible: Forging Resilience:

Remember that agonizing wait for a breakout that never materialized? Or that heart-stopping moment when a trade went south faster than a runaway train? Those are the moments that truly define us as traders. They teach us humility, the importance of patience, and the unwavering discipline to stick to our meticulously crafted trading plan. These experiences, while painful, are essential for building resilience and developing the emotional fortitude needed to succeed in the market.

Building Your Trading Empire: A Gradual Process:

This journey is not a sprint; it's a marathon. It's about incremental progress, about honing our skills, about learning from every victory and every setback. It's about building a strong foundation of knowledge and discipline that will serve us well for years to come.

Think of it as building a magnificent skyscraper. You don't simply snap your fingers and have it appear. You lay the groundwork, brick by painstaking brick, ensuring a solid foundation. Some days will be frustrating, the market may seem to conspire against you, and you might question whether it's all worth it. But other days, you'll witness the fruits of your labor, experiencing the exhilaration of a successful trade or the satisfaction of a well-executed strategy.

Staying the Course: The Power of Perseverance:

And remember, setbacks are inevitable. Doubt may creep in, fear may whisper in your ear. But as long as you stay focused, disciplined, and true to your trading plan, you can navigate these challenges and emerge stronger. Perseverance is the key to long-term success in trading.

The Journey Ahead: Embracing the Unknown:

So, go forth, my fellow traders. Embrace the challenge, embrace the learning process, and never stop striving for improvement. The journey may be long, and the path may be winding, but the rewards – both financial and personal – can be truly life-changing. The market is a dynamic and ever-changing environment. Embrace the uncertainty and be prepared to adapt and evolve.

Disclaimer: This information is for general knowledge and informational purposes only and does not constitute financial, investment, or other professional advice. Trading involves significant risk, and you could lose money. Always do your own research and consult with a qualified financial advisor before making any investment decisions.

Chapter 36: The Fintech Revolution and the Evolution of Finance

The world of finance is no longer a "boys' club" behind the marble pillars of Wall Street. For decades, the barrier to entry was high: you needed a broker, high commissions, and a landline phone just to place a trade. Today, that world is dead. It has been replaced by **Fintech** (Financial Technology), and for the retail trader, this is the ultimate equalizer.

From the Floor to the Fingerprint

In the past, if you wanted to buy a stock, your order had to be physically shouted on a trading floor. This created a delay between your decision and your execution. Today, Fintech has moved the entire stock exchange into your pocket.

Apps like **Robinhood, Webull, and Cash App** have pioneered "Commission-Free Trading." This is a game-changer for the side-hustle investor. When you don't have to pay $10 or $20 in fees just to enter a trade, you can start with smaller capital—allowing you to practice the principles of risk management without being drained by "the middleman."

The Democratization of Data

One of the biggest shifts in the evolution of finance is the speed of information. Previously, institutional investors (the "Big Dogs") had access to news and data hours or days before the public.

Now, with platforms like **TradingView** and real-time news aggregators, you have the same charts and the same data as the professionals. Fintech has stripped away the "information monopoly." If a CEO tweets or an earnings report drops, you see it at the same millisecond as a hedge fund manager in Manhattan. This allows us to apply the **KISS (Keep It Simple, Stupid)** principle effectively: the data is there, we just have to follow our plan.

Digital Assets and 24/7 Markets

Fintech didn't just change *how* we trade; it changed *when* and *what* we trade. The rise of **Cryptocurrency and Blockchain technology** has created a market that never sleeps. Unlike the NYSE, which closes in the afternoon, Fintech platforms allow you to manage your wealth 24 hours a day, 7 days a week.

For a father of seven or a veteran working a full-time job, this flexibility is vital. It means your "side hustle" doesn't have to fit into a 9-to-5 window. You can analyze, plan, and execute on your own schedule.

The New Bottom Line

The evolution of finance means that **opportunity is now a choice, not a privilege.** The tools are in your hands, the fees are gone, and the data is transparent. However, with this ease of access comes a greater need for the discipline we've discussed throughout this book. Just because it's easy to hit "Buy" on an app doesn't mean you should do it without a plan.

Fintech gives you the weapon; your trading plan is what teaches you how to aim.

Conclusion: Charting Your Course to Financial Freedom

As the founder of The Triangle Royalty Group LLC, I'm driven by a deep commitment to empowering individual investors like you to achieve lasting financial freedom. My passion for music profoundly shapes my investment philosophy. Just as music demands dedication, discipline, and a long-term perspective, so too does successful investing. Whether composing a symphony or allocating assets strategically, a solid understanding of fundamentals, combined with patience and discipline, is paramount. I believe in a thoughtful and deliberate approach, focusing on building a strong foundation and nurturing long-term growth, much like a musician meticulously crafting their sound.

Through The Triangle Royalty Group LLC, I aim to provide valuable insights and resources to help you navigate the market's complexities. My goal is to equip you with the tools and knowledge you need to build a robust financial foundation and achieve your unique investment objectives, whether it's retirement planning, saving for a down payment, or simply gaining greater financial independence.

Beyond the Ticker: A Holistic Approach to Wealth Building:

My personal philosophy on wealth building extends beyond the often-abstract world of stock tickers and ETFs. While these instruments can be powerful tools, I believe in grounding my financial strategy in tangible, real-world assets. This includes acquiring physical metals (gold, silver, etc.) as a hedge against uncertainty, securing land as a long-term investment, owning real estate that provides shelter and generates income, and even considering resources like firearms and ammunition, livestock, and the ability to cultivate my own food. These tangible assets represent a form of security and independence that complements the more fluid nature of market investments. I see trading not just as a means of generating profits, but as a tool to build a diversified portfolio that includes both digital and physical assets, creating a robust foundation for long-term financial well-being. Trading, therefore, becomes a strategic component in a larger plan – a way to generate income and acquire the tangible resources that provide a sense of stability and self-sufficiency. This holistic approach provides a buffer against market volatility and offers a sense of control over one's financial destiny.

The Unique Investment Journey: A Personal Symphony:

Just as Michael Jordan and Dennis Rodman were two vastly different basketball players, each excelling in their unique areas of expertise, every individual's investment journey is inherently personal and distinct. There's no magic formula, no one-size-fits-all approach that guarantees success. What works brilliantly for one person might be entirely unsuitable for another. This book has explored a variety of trading strategies and ideas related to stocks and ETFs, not as a rigid prescription or a set of commandments, but rather as a diverse menu of options. My intention is to spark your curiosity, to open doors to new possibilities, and to encourage you to delve deeper into the specific areas that resonate most strongly with your personality, your risk tolerance, and your financial goals. Consider your own strengths and weaknesses, your available time, and your comfort level with different investment vehicles.

Trading as Self-Discovery: A Mirror to Your Inner Self:

More than simply a guide to the mechanics of trading, I hope this book has also provided some insights into yourself. The world of trading, with its inherent challenges and emotional rollercoaster, can be a powerful tool for self-discovery. The more I trade, the more I learn not only about the intricacies of the markets, but also about my own strengths, my weaknesses, and my emotional triggers. Trading, like any demanding endeavor, can act as a mirror, reflecting aspects of your character and personality that you can then work on to become a more well-rounded and self-aware individual, both inside and outside the trading arena. It's a journey of continuous self-improvement, where the lessons learned in the market can often translate into positive changes in other areas of your life. The discipline, patience, and emotional control required for successful trading can be invaluable in other areas of life.

Breaking the Cycle: Empowering Future Generations:

Even if trading ultimately proves not to be your chosen path, I wholeheartedly encourage you to find something to invest in. You dedicate your time and energy to earning your money, and it's essential to make that money work for you. This is particularly crucial if you have children or plan to have them in the future. I know firsthand the challenges of navigating the complexities of the adult financial world without a solid foundation. After graduating high school, I felt woefully unprepared for the monetary realities of independent life. We weren't taught these fundamental principles in school, and my parents, while incredibly hardworking and supportive, may not have had the financial literacy to fully equip me with the knowledge I needed. This lack of financial education is a common experience for many, and it's a cycle that we have the power to break. By investing in your own financial education, you are not only securing your future but also empowering future generations.

The Power of Knowledge: Taking Control of Your Destiny:

But the empowering truth is that this essential information is readily available. We live in an age of unprecedented access to knowledge. You have the opportunity to change the financial trajectory of your family for generations to come, simply by committing to lifelong learning and taking proactive steps to improve your financial literacy. Trading, when approached with discipline, knowledge, and a long-term perspective, is a valuable skill that can serve you well throughout your life. As I've emphasized throughout this book, trading has been a part of human history for centuries, and while the specific tools and techniques may change, the underlying principles of supply, demand, and value remain remarkably consistent. Embrace this opportunity to learn and grow.

Your Personal Quest: A Call to Action:

Ultimately, your investment journey is just that – yours. It's a deeply personal quest for financial empowerment, and it's a journey that should be approached with intention, a thirst for knowledge, and a crystal-clear understanding of your own individual goals, risk tolerance, and core values. I encourage you to embrace the challenge, explore the vast array of possibilities that the financial world offers, and take decisive control of your financial destiny. The world of investing is waiting, and with the right preparation, the right mindset, and a commitment to continuous growth, you can achieve your financial dreams and build a future of security and opportunity for yourself and your loved ones. Start today. Even small steps can lead to significant progress over time.

It would not be right without leaving you a few websites for you to use for continued learning. I am not getting any compensation from any of the websites listed. I use or have used most of these products before and trust them as being credible.

1. **Fidelity: Excellent all-around platform with strong research tools, low costs, and a wide range of investment options. Great for both beginners and experienced investors.**

2. **Charles Schwab: Similar to Fidelity, Schwab offers a user-friendly experience, extensive research, and a huge selection of no-load mutual funds.**

3. **E*TRADE: Another solid choice for beginners, E*TRADE provides good educational resources and a user-friendly platform, especially for mobile investing.**

4. **Vanguard: If you're primarily focused on low-cost index funds and ETFs, Vanguard is a top choice. They are known for their investor-owned structure and commitment to low fees.**

For Active Traders & Options Traders:

5. **Interactive Brokers: This platform is geared towards more advanced traders, offering a wide range of trading tools, global market access, and very competitive pricing.**

6. **tastytrade: If you're specifically interested in options trading, tastytrade is a great option. Their platform is designed for active traders and offers unique features like a "follow" feed to see what other traders are doing.**

7. **Robinhood: Popular among younger investors due to its simple and mobile-first interface.**

8. **Webull: Similar to Robinhood, Webull offers a user-friendly platform with some more advanced features. It's a good option for those who want a mobile-focused experience with some extra tools.**

For Research & Education:

9. **Morningstar: A leading source of investment research and analysis. They offer in-depth reports, ratings, and screeners to help you make informed investment decisions.**

10. The Motley Fool: Provides a wealth of investing information, including stock recommendations, educational articles, and community forums.

Personal picks
verfiedinvesting.com
thetechnicaltraders.com
tradingview.com
stocktwits.com[1]

1. http://stocktwits.com

.Advanced Analysis Dashboard Template

Metric	Calculation / Description	Result	Notes
Total Trades	Count of all recorded trades.	100	N/A
Win Rate	(Number of Winning Trades / Total Trades) x 100	[Formula: Enter Percentage]	Should be calculated periodically (e.g., every 25 trades) to assess consistency.
Average Win ($)	Sum of P&L ($) for winning trades / Count of winning trades	[Enter Currency]	Helps determine the strength of your winning trades.
Average Loss ($)	Sum of P&L ($) for losing trades / Count of losing trades	[Enter Currency]	Helps determine the size of your losing trades.
Expectancy	(Win Rate * Avg. Win) - (Loss Rate * Avg. Loss)	[Enter Currency]	**If positive, your strategy has a statistical edge.**
Maximum Drawdown	The largest peak-to-trough decline during the 100-trade cycle.	[Enter Currency / Percentage]	A key risk management metric.
Max Consecutive Losses	The longest string of losing trades in the period.	[Enter Number]	A critical mental fortitude metric.

——-Performance by Strategy

Use this table to analyze which of your "Arrangements" (strategies) are the most effective.

Strategy Name	Total Trades	Win Rate (%)	Avg R-Multiple	Notes
Harmonic Convergence Breakout	[Enter Count]	[Enter Percentage]	[Enter Number]	
Fibonacci Retracement Swing	[Enter Count]	[Enter Percentage]	[Enter Number]	
[Add Your Own Strategy]				

The Conductor's Rehearsal: Your First 100 Trades

In trading, a single "at-bat" doesn't define your average. You need a consistent sample size to prove your strategy has a statistical edge. Use this checklist for every trade to ensure you stay in the "rhythm" of discipline:

1. Identify the Setup: Does this trade align with my "Playbook" (e.g., Harmonic Convergence or Fibonacci Retracement)?

2. Check the Catalysts: Can I identify 2–3 specific reasons (fundamental or technical) why this price will move?

3. Find the Tempo (Position Sizing): Have I calculated my position size so I am not risking more than 1–2% of my total capital?

4. Set the Failsafe: Is my Hard Stop-Loss entered into the system to protect my "home-front" capital?

5. Define the Crescendo: Do I have a clear Profit Target based on the chart's geometry, or am I trading on "hope"?

6. Journal the Performance: Have I recorded my emotional state (Fear, Greed, or Neutral) and the trade rationale in my journal?

About the Author

Marcus Dewayne Green Sr. is the founder of **The Triangle Royalty Group LLC (TRG)** and a dedicated strategist in the world of retail trading and private equity. A veteran of the **United States Army**, Marcus applies the **KISS (Keep It Simple, Stupid)** principle to every aspect of his financial life, believing that clarity and discipline are the ultimate equalizers in a complex market.

Marcus's journey into finance began in 2007, driven by a desire to break the cycle of financial instability and provide a "sovereign" future for his family. As a father of seven—including three biological children and four currently in the adoption process—he understands the high stakes of being a sole provider. His "600 Dollar Lesson" remains a cornerstone of his teaching, serving as a powerful reminder that risk management is not just a strategy, but a necessity for survival.

A lifelong musician with a catalog of over 200 compositions, Marcus views the stock market not as a chaotic gamble, but as a **Market Symphony**. He specializes in **Swing Trading**, utilizing a high-conviction approach that merges 85% technical analysis with 15% fundamental grit.

Today, Marcus lives in the **Phoenix/Casa Grande** area of Arizona with his wife of 18 years, Michelle. Through his writing, music, and the development of the **TRG "Command Center"** application, he is committed to empowering a new generation of "Sovereign Traders" to conduct their own path to financial independence.

Market Symphony: A Musician's Guide to Trading Stocks, ETFs, and Digital Assets

Marcus Dewayne Green Sr. learned the hard way that the market doesn't reward "hunches" or "luck"—it rewards a plan. After losing a significant portion of his capital just days before rent was due, he stopped "playing" the market and started studying its mechanics.

Market Symphony is the KISS (Keep It Simple, Stupid) guide for the modern retail trader. It is written for the people who are the "only chance" for their families—those who need supplemental income without the complexity of a finance degree. Drawing on his experience as a U.S. Army veteran, a father of seven, and the founder of **The Triangle Royalty Group**, Marcus provides a disciplined "score" for navigating the financial landscape.

Your family's future is the ultimate "why." It's time to stop the noise and start the performance.

www.ingramcontent.com/pod-product-compliance
Lightning Source LLC
LaVergne TN
LVHW082337200926
848481LV00012B/3371